D0385615

WOMEN *in the* OLD TESTAMENT

THE MACMILLAN COMPANY
NEW YORK · BOSTON · CHICAGO · DALLAS
ATLANTA · SAN FRANCISCO

WOMEN in the OLD TESTAMENT

Twenty Psychological Portraits

BY NORAH LOFTS

THE MACMILLAN COMPANY
New York · 1950

The quotation on page 77 is from "Sir Richard's Song" from *Puck of Pook's Hill* by Rudyard Kipling. Copyright, 1905, 1906, by Rudyard Kipling. Reprinted by permission of Mrs. George Bambridge and Doubleday & Company, Inc.

The quotation on page 122 is from "En-dor" from *The Years Between* by Rudyard Kipling. Copyright, 1914, 1919, by Rudyard Kipling. Reprinted by permission of Mrs. George Bambridge and Doubleday & Company, Inc.

The several quotations from *Requiem* by Humbert Wolfe, copyright, 1927, by Humbert Wolfe, are reprinted by permission of Doubleday & Company, Inc.

Printed in the United States of America
By The Haddon Craftsmen, Inc., Scranton, Pa.

This, the last of my books to have the benefit of his help and advice during its making, is dedicated to the memory of my husband,

GEOFFREY LOFTS 1905-1948

"Dear, dead women, with such hair, too."

(Browning)

Foreword

There was once, in the journalistic world, a slogan which ran—"Women are always news!" and even now, in the nineteen-forties it does not seem to be quite outworn. The very existence of the series to which this book belongs, "Women in . . ." pre-supposes that there is something automatically interesting, almost automatically romantic, in merely belonging to the female sex, and that when any woman engages in any specific activity outside strictly functional ones, more people are interested in the process and in the result than they would be if the same process were followed, the same result achieved, by a man.

The only valid reason that I can see for this focussing of interest upon the female is that in any assembly attention is always directed—if only for a moment—towards the latest arrival; and Woman arrived late upon the outer, public scene, just as she arrived late—if we believe the story of the Creation—upon the actual planet. Men have done and thought and achieved things until doing and thinking and achieving have become commonplace; then some woman does, thinks, achieves, and interest immediately revives. It is not entirely flattering to Woman; a little reminiscent of Dr. Johnson's comment upon the performing dog. However, that cannot be helped; and the author of "Women in the Old Testament" together with those of "Women in Art" and "Women in Crime" and all the other exploiters of this curious interest in the female, must be grateful that the general, if unacknowledged, opinion of women is so low that the words "Woman Sweeps Chimney" would make an arresting headline even in these days of paper shortage.

So here is a book, written by a woman, about a group of people who have nothing in common save their sex and the fact that their names or their stories happen to be included in what is one

 *Contents* 

Chapter 1

THE GENERAL BACKGROUND

To the humanitarian the test of the degree of civilisation reached by any community of people is not its measure of material progress, the magnificence of its buildings, the extent of its conquests, the cleanliness of its water supply, but the amount of consideration shown to its weaker members and amongst these weaker members all women—if they are performing the natural functions of woman—must willy-nilly, rank themselves at one time or another.

Any woman who bears a child must, for some weeks at least, be at the mercy of circumstances, dependent upon some man or upon the community: and afterwards, if she applies herself conscientiously to rearing her child her out-of-home activities are limited and some measure of economic dependence remains. Upon this fact and upon an inferior equipment of muscle and brawn the long story of woman's subjugation is rooted, and from the same root spring the injustices which range from the acceptance of a "double standard" of moral behaviour to anomalies over the owning of property. So in studying and testing a people, or a period by the question: "How did they treat their weak?" we must allow the collective word to include the women with the lunatics, the very poor, the mentally or physically infirm.

From such a test the Jews of the Old Testament emerge honourably. The very fact that one can sit down today and study the lives and characters of these Old Testament women proves that while they were alive they were regarded as human beings in their own right, not as mere appurtenances of men. They are given their names and allowed their idiosyncracies, and any part that they played in the making of Israel's history is credited to them. In this the Old Testament differs enormously and wonderfully from the early history of other races in which the women only matter because some man loved them, or because, from behind the purdah curtains, they exerted a mild, indirect influence over some man's decisions. Deborah was married to Lapidoth and Jael to Heber, but they are both admitted to be more important and influential than their husbands. The only account of indirect, purdah influence in the whole of the Old Testament comes in the story of Esther, who was Queen of Persia, not of Israel. And her story is in sharp contrast with those of Jezebel and Michal. They also lived in palaces, but there is no hint in their stories of the segregation of women or of silence in the presence of men.

One must conclude that the Jewish women were more free and less regarded as chattels than other Eastern women of their time. And it is worth noticing that in the very early days, when the law was being hammered out upon the anvil of emergency, the daughters of Zelophedad came to Moses and voiced a trenchant question. "Why," they demanded, "should the name of our father be done away from among his family because he hath no sons? Give unto us therefore a possession among the brethren of our father." If ever male priority of inheritance were challenged it was then; and by how many disinherited women has that question been echoed? Moses, the law-giver, consulted Jehovah who gave a plain pronouncement. "Thou shalt speak unto the children of Israel saying–If a man die and have no son then ye shall cause his inheritance to pass unto his daughter." As a blow for the rights of women it was incomplete and inconclusive; its uniqueness lies in its assumption that in some circumstances some women could have some rights; and it is thus well ahead of contemporary law.

From such an apparently mild and reasonable dictum to the emancipation of women in the Western hemisphere centuries later is a far cry and one hesitates to press a fanciful theory too hard. But it is fact that the women of the West have long had, and still have, a freedom unknown in the East, and it is also a fact that St. Paul, on his missionary journey turned to the West, not to the East. The facts may not be unrelated. It is true that St. Paul carried Christianity, not Judaism, but it is equally true that amongst the accusations brought against Christ, that of attempting to emancipate women did not take a place. So what Paul carried *may* have been not the implicit Christian dictate with regard to female status, but the inherited, almost unconscious, implied dictate of his race. And it would be possible, if controversial, to offer the idea that the freedom of the modern Western woman is the legacy far derived, long-ripening, of Israel.

In looking at the background of the women of the Old Testament one must accept the fact that polygamy was the rule rather than the exception. Distasteful as it may seem to us, polygamy serves a useful purpose in places where, and at times when, a nation is establishing itself, when conditions of life are harsh, expectation of life short and the need for many children imperative. The Jews distinguished sharply between polygamy and adultery. David had many wives and more concubines but only his association with the married woman, Bathsheba, was regarded as adulterous. Despite polygamy, prostitution, "the oldest profession," was not unknown, though it is worth noting that neither of the prostitutes included in this series was a Jewess; Rahab was a Canaanite, Delilah a Philistine. Virginity was highly valued, as it is admittedly by most primitive peoples, and less openly but no less surely by more sophisticated communities. The penalty for violation was death. A newly wedded woman proved not to be virgin was in danger of being returned to her family, a flawed, unsaleable thing, doomed to spend the rest of her life in the service of women more respectable or more cautious.

The domestic background was simple and similar to that of many "backward" countries today. The women were kept busy spinning and weaving and dyeing the cloth for the family's clothing, gathering fuel, gleaning, winnowing, cooking, bearing their babies and tending the sick and old. During the nomadic period of Israel's history they lived in tents, cheek by jowl with the flocks and herds which composed their wealth; later they lived in houses of clay or stone according to their circumstances; flat-topped houses for the drying of fruit and grain and flax.

Their lives sound immensely, almost enviably simple; but I believe—and I write in that belief—that life, the real business of living alters very little. I believe

Chapter 2

SARAH AND HAGAR

AUTHORIZED VERSION: *Genesis 16:1-23:20*

"Let Hell afford the pavement for her Heaven."
(*Henry Cust*: NON NOBIS)

The story of these two women is the first in the Bible—with the exception of the story of the Garden of Eden—in which women figure largely; and it is a sad story because it concerns itself with one of Fortune's favourite daughters and one of Fortune's step-children. Sarah moved easily and triumphantly through life, blessed with beauty, with her husband's enduring love, blessed too in her own nature which could turn a disadvantage into an asset, and laugh where tears would have been justified. Sarah has the sun on her; and by contrast Hagar's shadowed fate shows darker.

They were both very feminine women, and both had faults; and out of their femininity and their characters the details of the story take their shape, but the broader pattern of the drama was an imposed thing, a matter of time and environment, divorced from the individualities of the women concerned. Sarah and Hagar came into conflict through the dictates of their own temperaments and moods, but they were both victims of a system, and any other two women placed in their position would have been forced to work out a drama similar in essence, differing only in non-essentials.

Sarah was the wife of the patriarch Abraham; and she must have been an exceptionally beautiful and attractive woman. The chroniclers of the Book of Genesis were dealing with high and important matters, but they spared time for a specific mention of her beauty. She was "a fair woman to look upon." Abraham was married to her before he set out on his wanderings, and when he sojourned for a time in Egypt he feared that in that sophisticated, wealthy, beauty-loving society Sarah's beauty might lead to trouble. Someone important might covet it, and kill off the inconvenient husband.

So Abraham proposed, and Sarah accepted, a rather curious plan. They were to pretend to be brother and sister; and this plan, which seems tantamount to inviting men to desire her, resulted in Sarah being taken into the house of the reigning Pharaoh; for even in Egypt, where lovely women from all nations were gathered, Sarah's beauty had caused a minor sensation; the princes of Egypt found her "very fair" and commandeered her for Pharaoh's harem. Abraham, as the brother of the new and dazzlingly beautiful favourite, received substantial presents, sheep and oxen, and asses and camels and man-servants and maid-servants. It may even have been that he had cherished some such thought when he said to Sarah, "Say thou art my sister that it may be well with me for thy sake . . ."

Pharaoh never enjoyed Sarah's beauty. The text reads, "the Lord plagued Pharaoh and his house with great plagues," and by some mental process not explained to us Pharaoh associated the plagues with the latest addition to his harem, and discovered the truth, and sent for Abraham and asked, reasonably enough, "Why didst thou not tell me that she was thy wife?" And he said, "Take her and go thy way." But he refrained from demanding that the presents should be returned, and when Abraham took his wife and went his way he also took the nucleus of the wealth upon which the whole family and the whole tribe and the whole nation of Israel was to be founded. Pretty faces have often proved destructive; very seldom has a pretty face led to such solid construction.

Amongst the spoils which Abraham and Sarah brought out of Egypt was a young maid-servant called Hagar, who was to become the mother of Ishmael. She was also to be a weapon to the hand, and then a thorn in the side, and last a bitter memory in the mind, of Sarah.

It is likely too, that Sarah brought out of Egypt something intangible, but of value. For she had been where few desert women had been, into the harem of Pharaoh's palace where there were gathered not only some of the loveliest women in the whole of the known world but also a vast mass of esoteric feminine knowledge. All day long, day after day, these women in the palace at the very hub of the world, beauties from Greece and Phoenicia, from Arabia and Ethiopia, had no other study, no other exercise than the art of seductiveness, and even the briefest stay in the very heart and centre of female art and fashion must have left its mark upon the beautiful unsophisticated nomad woman who had come out of the desert and who returned to it. Sarah must have returned to her husband knowing all that there was to know about cosmetics, and the tiring of the hair, the perfuming and adorning of the body and the other, less obvious ways, of attracting and holding a man's attention.

And she needed it all. Not immediately, when as a young woman she was restored to her husband and they could gloat together, not only over their reunion but over the wealth which their brief separation had brought them. But presently, as year followed year, it began to seem plain that the greatest curse of Eastern womanhood was Sarah's; she was barren. So loved, so lovely, but childless.

What made the situation strange and particularly tragic was that the God whom Abraham served, this new, incomprehensible God who had ordered him to leave his own country and his own people and who now dictated all his actions and movements, had promised, definitely promised, that Abraham's seed should be as the dust of the earth, "so that if any man can number the dust of the earth then shall thy seed also be numbered." But the years passed, and though the flocks and the herds increased, though Abraham still loved his wife, still believed in God's promise, there was no child, no son.

Abraham bore the disappointment well, even a little peculiarly. There is no sign that he ever reproached Sarah, though then the blame for a childless marriage was invariably borne by the wife, nor did he, in that wildly polygamous age, ever attempt to take another wife or a concubine. He had a favourite servant, a kind of steward called Eliezer, and he seemed placidly resigned to leaving all his wealth to him. Only once, in secret communion with his God did Abraham betray his grief, and point out, with a kind of gentle irony that he, to whom was promised the progeny from whom a great nation should spring, had for his heir only a servant. And God replied that what He had promised should come about and that Abraham's own son should succeed him.

And almost at once, so hard upon the heels of that renewal of promise, Sarah moved. It is possible that Abraham reported to her this latest conversation with his God, and that she was frightened lest under its inspiration he might take another wife who would bear a child and thus supercede her. Or it may have been that she was now prepared to accept the fact of her barrenness and realized that since Abraham had remained faithful to her it was incumbent upon her to suggest some expedient. For whatever reason she looked about her and saw that her bondwoman, Hagar, had grown to maturity. So she offered Hagar to Abraham.

Hagar could never really be her mistress' rival, though she bore a hundred sons. She belonged to Sarah, and any child she bore could be taken away at birth and reared as Sarah's. That was the law. When Sarah made her suggestion she said, "It may be that I may obtain children by her." But there is no mention of what the suggestion cost the proud, lovely, beloved woman, no mention of the innumerable disappointments, the hopes, the tears in the night, the prayers, the final despair.

Hagar, of course, had no say in the matter. She was a piece of property, so subservient, so personally negligible that the thought of Abraham's consorting with her would occasion Sarah the least possible pang. And a further antidote to jealousy would lie in the fact that Abraham's possession of the slave girl had been Sarah's suggestion. Had he been attracted to her for herself he would have shown some sign. Hagar, in fact, was only the shadowy projection of Sarah; another self, another body with a womb which might prove fertile.

Romanticism would like to believe that Hagar had, for long years past, adored her master and welcomed this unexpected chance of intimacy with him. But the facts of the story refute the idea. Had Hagar loved Abraham she would have borne with Sarah's bullying during her pregnancy, and later behaved with more tact and cunning, caring nothing for Sarah, caring for nothing so long as she was where she could see Abraham and hear his voice every day. So the romantic thought must perish, and we must see the relationship between Hagar and her master as Sarah saw it, a cool, matter-of-fact expedient, a physical adjustment with no sentimental significance, a thing which left Sarah's position entirely unassailed. But sad—sad for Hagar.

The slave girl quickened, and imperceptibly everything became changed. Sarah had given her bondmaid to Abraham in the hope that she would bear a child, but perhaps she had not fully reckoned upon the consequences. For one thing the blame for the childlessness of the marriage—never certain until now, since Abraham had been monogamous—was laid squarely upon Sarah. And Abraham, however perfunctory his embraces had been, could now hardly avoid seeing in the slave girl the instrument by whom God's promise was to be fulfilled. But the greatest change of all was that which took place in Hagar herself. Unnoticed, unconsidered, little higher in status than an animal, she had spent her life at Sarah's beck and call, and now she had done something that her mistress had failed to do.

Hagar must be blamed, in large measure, for the unpleasantness that ensued. Unless it was that Sarah had been extremely guileful and anxious to prove Abraham's impotence she must have anticipated the situation and been prepared to face it; but she had counted upon the Egyptian girl's meekness; and that had suddenly disappeared. As soon as the slave girl was pregnant she despised her mistress and the scorn showed in every word, every glance, every gesture. Aggressive self-importance is the legacy of past underprivilege, and Hagar had been a slave all her life. The utmost reaches of her ambition would be to attract her master's attention and to bear him a child; now she had done so; and she may not have known of Sarah's connivance.

For Sarah, obviously she had no affection at all. If she had she would have pitied her, allowed her to share, vicariously, in her blessed state; or kept herself out of sight, trying not to emphasise the hurt. But Hagar must have been jealous of Sarah over many years. Sarah had everything save one thing; while Hagar had nothing; and now Hagar had the one thing which all women desired beyond all else. So she flaunted herself and became insolent and overbearing.

But if Sarah had overestimated Hagar's meekness, Hagar had misunderstood Sarah completely. There was a vast humiliation waiting to be accepted and mourned over, but Sarah ignored it. She is not an altogether admirable character but it is impossible to withhold admiration from her at this moment. So many women would have turned inwards upon themselves, become sly, lachrymose, deceitful even to themselves. Sarah was open and honest and forthright.

She knew—she could not help but know—what the promise of a child meant to any man, especially to a man in Abraham's position; she knew that she herself had failed in the most fundamental sphere of womanhood; she knew that Hagar was pregnant because she herself had suggested that Abraham consort with her. But all that meant nothing. Personality triumphed over circumstance, and risking cold reason, snub, sneer, with God and man and every convention ranged against her, she yet took the offensive; she went to Abraham and complained of Hagar's behaviour to her. It must have taken superb courage, superb confidence. What might not Abraham have said—"You yourself suggested this." "God promised me a family and you are barren." "If you cannot live with Hagar, who is to bear my child, you can go."

He said none of these things. He had been promised children. His wife was barren. He had, at his wife's suggestion, begotten a child upon a bondmaiden and it seemed as though through the bondmaiden the promise might be fulfilled; yet when Sarah complained that Hagar had been insolent he said, "Behold, thy maid is in thy hand, do to her as it pleaseth thee." Not one man in a thousand would have given that answer; not one woman in a thousand could have elicited it. It is a triumph unrivalled in the whole history of marriage.

So Sarah began to deal "hardly" with Hagar. She may even have physically ill-used her. And Hagar, simple, primitive woman, growing heavy with Abraham's child, would look to him for support and protection and find none. Nothing had changed after all; she was still Sarah's bondwoman though within her Sarah's husband's seed matured. A bitter thing to face.

The time came when Hagar could face it no more, when she felt that life under Sarah's roof was not to be endured. So she fled away into the desert. And there, we are told, she was visited by an angel who told her that her son should be the father of a great nation, and that she must return to her mistress and be submissive.

An angel? Or wishful thinking? How vast and bare did the desert loom? How heavily did the child weigh? Food, water, help in the hour of travail, could the desert provide these? An angel—or plain reason?

She went back to the place where there was food and comfort, soft skins to lie upon and hands to help in the critical hour. And there she bore Ishmael, Abraham's only child; his heir, unless, as seemed extremely improbable, Sarah should yet produce a son.

Sarah's behaviour and attitude towards Ishmael is not described but it would be safe to imagine that she took an avid, bitter interest in him. Perhaps then she realised, for the first time, the full extent of her loss; as she searched his face for traces of resemblance to Abraham, ignoring any likeness to Hagar; as she saw Abraham's pleasure in him, as she watched the chubby lines of babyhood lengthen out into the incomparable beauty that lives for a time in the body of every little boy. How could she help but think that if the slave girl's son could be such a treasure, and so beautiful, her own would have been immeasurably more precious, indescribably more lovely.

In the presence of Hagar she probably ignored him, and then, in his mother's absence, spoke to him kindly, gave him tit-bits, and corrected his manners, remembering that he was to be Abraham's heir. Possibly some of her later spite was seeded during this period when every time she saw the child, or heard his voice, she must remember that Hagar had borne him and yet must look and listen and think—ah, if only you were mine!

But Sarah's weak moments were known only to herself. Like a tree that bears bright blossom, but no fruit, she stood proud and lovely still, making what beauty she could out of her barren autumn. And thirteen years passed, thirteen years during which Ishmael was reared and treated as Abraham's heir; years during which all, even the wildest, hope of Sarah's becoming a mother, perished. Yet still, when God communed with Abraham, He reiterated that old promise, that Abraham's wife should bear a son and that that son should become the founder of a great people.

And then Abraham received that mysterious visit which we commemorate when we speak of entertaining angels unawares. He offered to three chance strangers the open-handed hospitality that is the rule in the desert and on frontiers and in sparsely populated places, and then discovered they were Jehovah's emissaries, bringing warning of the fate of Sodom and Gomorrah, the wicked cities of the plain.

It *is* possible to rationalise Hagar's angel. Not that one wishes to do so, or that it is necessary to do so. But Hagar's angel told her nothing except what her common sense and her jealousy of Sarah might not have invented. It was common sense to go back to the tents and it was natural, since she had grown up hearing about Sarah's son who was to be the father of a nation that she should make a similar claim for hers. But Abraham's angels are not so easily disposed of. They foretold the destruction of the cities of the plain, which did not come about for some days; and another event nine months ahead.

For to Sarah, who was listening in the tent door, womanlike, to hear and see what was going on, they promised something almost as dramatic and improbable as that fire from heaven should consume Sodom and Gomorrah; they said that she should bear a son. And she knew—who better—that her child-bearing time was past. So she laughed.

In that laughter more of the woman whom we glimpsed in that complaint to Abraham about Hagar's behaviour, is revealed. One understands why Abraham loved her. So many women would have wept, seeing the pity of their case, Sarah saw the irony of it and laughed. It may have been, it probably was, bitter laughter; but it was laughter in the face of an evil fate, laughter in the very face of God. Nor did it pass unmarked. It provoked Jehovah to ask Abraham, "Wherefore did Sarah laugh? . . . Is anything too hard for the Lord?"

The question of age must here be faced. Other stories in the Old Testament seem to call for a certain wariness, but this demands either complete credulity or some cool dissection. Sarah, we are told, was ninety and Abraham a hundred years old at the time of Isaac's conception. Were they full years, the years we know? And there is—if you can bear it—a clue to an answer in the child Ishmael. Some little time before he is said to be thirteen years old; one allows nine months for the gestation of Isaac, and a little time more for his weaning, and for trouble between the two mothers to come to a head, and that makes Ishmael hard on fourteen years old—if not quite fourteen—when he and Hagar were driven out into the desert. Yet Hagar, we read, "Cast the child under one of the shrubs," and walked away in order that she might not witness his death. Now a boy of fourteen, reared as Ishmael had been, to nomadic life in the desert, would have borne, one feels, thirst and fatigue as well as a female house slave, and would certainly present a problem when it came to casting under shrubs. Was he fourteen years old by our measure? Was Abraham a hundred and was Sarah ninety when the long-delayed hope was fulfilled? It is not for me to say. People wiser, people I respect, accept the ages as they are given. I cherish a secret desire to halve them. Sarah at forty-five might well be astonished to find herself with child for the first time in her life—and Ishmael at six and a half or seven might have flagged before his mother and been lain by her in the shade of a shrub.

But all that is really irrelevant to the story. Nine months after the angels' visit Sarah bore her son and called him Isaac, which means Laughter. And then Hagar knew that her son was deposed. Despite his seniority and the promise which had since his birth seemed to rest upon his young head, Ishmael became merely a slave's child, far lower in the scale of importance than a second or third or tenth legitimate son. It was a bitter thing to accept.

All the evidence points to Hagar having been a woman of simple mental processes; her pregnancy had exalted her and her reaction had been primitive, almost automatic. She was unperceptive. But the unperceptive are not necessarily insensitive where their own feelings are concerned; and it was now impossible for her to avoid the realisation that her motherhood, the thing which had crowned her life and lifted her—since her child was also her master's—out of her state of bondage, had now lost all but its purely personal significance. So far as Sarah and Abraham were concerned it might never have happened. While Ishmael had been the heir, Hagar had been, however much Sarah might pretend otherwise, the mother of the heir. Special, unique. Now that was all ended. Isaac's first wail upon the waiting air put Hagar back in her place, her place of bondage.

And Sarah, "who having much, had this more given," was not, alas, the woman to conceal her sense of triumph, to be gentle, pitiful. For as bondage had weighed upon Hagar, barrenness had weighed upon Sarah; each had, in turn, exploited the other's disadvantage. Hagar was a slave, Sarah a wife, then Hagar was a mother, Sarah childless. Now Sarah had a child in her arms and fourteen years of bitter envy to avenge. A hideous warfare of jealousy and hatred began to wage between the two women, so closely confined within the living space of the tents and bound together by their dependence upon the man who had fathered both their children. Usually, in literature, the purdah curtain hides this, the darkest side of polygamy; but here we can see each woman thrusting forward her child for notice, greedy for a sign of favour, cruelly angered if such favour shines for a moment upon the other's child. Ishmael, well-grown, trained by you, Abraham, responsive, intelligent, almost a man, how can you compare him with that brat wailing in its cradle, frail, imma-

he had, all those years ago, been a little shocked that Sarah should have taken his permission to do as she would with her slave girl, so literally, and to have made her life so wretched that she ran away. Perhaps all through the ensuing years he had watched Sarah growing harder and more arbitrary. And perhaps on that first occasion his feelings had been complicated by pity for his childless wife, and he had been anxious not to underline her failure by a show of consideration for the woman who was to bear his child. Now there was no reason to feel sorry for Sarah, she had her son in her arms and, to a man of the patriarchal age, there would seem to be no very vital reason why the two women upon whom he had begotten progeny should not dwell together in some sort of amity, and the two boys grow up together and eventually inherit, in strictly proportionate measure, the property which he was accumulating. It was so in a thousand families all around. Most of all "the thing was very grievous in Abraham's sight because of his son . . ." that is, Ishmael. The boy was, after all, his son, had been for years his only son; he had come to an age where his company was entertaining, the evidence of his budding mind engaging, his wish to be near his father flattering. The fond ties of time, of watched growth, of shared experience, were not so easily broken.

So Abraham hesitated and was grieved. But he discussed the matter with his God, as once before he had discussed his childlessness, and again he received a comfortable answer. The promise of that great nation was to be fulfilled through Isaac, the son of Sarah, therefore Abraham might concede to her wish. As for Ishmael, there was no need to worry about him, he too would father a nation because he was Abraham's son.

One wonders if Hagar were cognisant, or suspicious of, the underground currents which were to influence her destiny. Did she know how virulently Sarah hated her; or why Abraham's countenance was so grieved? Did she try—not perhaps to ingratiate herself with her hated mistress and rival, but to exploit Ishmael's power over his father? And how did Sarah endure this time of hesitation upon her husband's part? Thinking—last time he had no doubts, no scruples, now he is undecided . . . and turn for comfort and the restoration of complacency towards Isaac's cradle.

Abraham himself broke the news to Hagar and on the day of her departure rose up very early in the morning to set her on her way. He hoped that an early start, before the heat of the day threatened, and the bread and the water with which he loaded her might ensure that before nightfall she and the boy would reach the shelter of some oasis in the desert.

It must have been a curious parting between a man and a woman who had known the closest intimacy without feeling anything warmer than kindness. And there was between them the shadow of Sarah, warm in her bed with her baby beside her; still sleeping, or waking only to feel a thrill of triumph and then to sleep again. The thought of her lay heavy upon them both, this pair whom her will had thrust into one bed, and who were now, by her caprice, to take leave of one another forever.

Then Abraham turned to the child and one can imagine his hands lingering upon the strong active little body that he had begotten; his fatherly heart yearning towards the responsive, loving young heart which must be thrust away. Isaac in time would grow, but it was this little brown hand which had initiated him to fatherhood. This was the first-born, the provoker of feelings never to be repeated. And out of his very emotion at the parting, Abraham could derive resignation. God–and Sarah–were right. The real, the glorious future lay with Isaac and it was better that there should be no confusion, not even in the heart.

Ishmael, half-informed by, yet not fully understanding, all the bitter words which his mother had spoken during the last hours, would be sad at parting from the man who was his father and who had always treated him with kindness. One sees him clinging, looking backwards, waving, snatching a last glance, puzzled, confused, full of the momentary yet anguished misery of the young.

Hagar walked forwards with a face–and heart–of stone. A glimpse of her mind at that moment would have been a shattering insight into slavery's devilment. She was a woman, a live, sentient thing compounded of mind and spirit and body as other women were. But because Sarah had pleased Pharaoh, and Hagar had been a bondmaid, she had never been anything but a lump of wax in her mistress' hand. Shaped to mating, shaped to motherhood and now cast aside. She had conceived and she had borne, as the animals of the herds conceived and bore; now she was being driven out as no animal was ever driven, to perish in the wilderness. Heavy at first the bundle of bread and the bottle of water upon her brown shoulder; heavy at first the heart within her breast. Then light, perilously light, the outer load, and changed the one within. The bread is eaten and the water drunk, and the thought of Sarah and Isaac and Abraham and the sense of injustice and all the bitterness vanish in the flood of sheer physical panic. The moment came when nothing mattered, nothing was worthy of consideration compared with the imminence of death. Ishmael collapsed and she left him under a clump of camel thorn and staggered a little further that she might not have the agony of watching him die. And then she sat down and wept. But it was not—we read—her voice to which God hearkened, it was the voice of the child. (Poor Hagar, doomed never to be noticed for herself.) And the angelic voice spoke to her again and she opened her eyes and there was the well of water and she filled the bottle; and her life and that of Ishmael were saved.

So Sarah was rid of Hagar. But the day came when Abraham announced that it was God's will that Isaac, now an attractive, well-grown little boy, should be offered as a sacrifice upon an altar of stone. Then, for the first time in all her long life of dominance, Sarah knew what it was to be impotent. Not all her tears, her pleadings, her frenzy, could move Abraham from what he conceived to be his duty. So Sarah, who had known all those barren years when a son seemed the most desirable thing in the world, Sarah who had renounced hope and then, late in time, known a miraculous fulfillment, was compelled to take her boy in her arms and kiss him for the last time, to stand in the tent door and watch his innocent, unsuspecting departure for the mountains of Moriah, knowing that in that far place the child was to die, bloodily, by his father's own hand; that the flesh and the bone formed from her own, were to be consumed in the sacrificial flame, and that Abraham would come back alone, a broken, sonless man.

Sarah did not, in that awful hour, think of Hagar and her son, sacrificed upon another altar; there would be no room in her mind for anything but her own searing grief. But that was sharp and bitter and complete enough to have satisfied even Hagar, could she have known about it. For Sarah that day was a rebel against God, dark as Lucifer, knowing the same sickening fall.

Her agony was longer than Hagar's. Hagar had said, "Let me not see the death of the child." It was three days' journey to Moriah, and three back, so for six days Sarah saw nothing but the death of her child. Six days of unmitigated torment. And then Abraham returned with some babbled story about a voice and a ram caught in the thicket—how could she give it any heed? For Isaac was with him, alive, whole, alive! For the second time a miracle had filled Sarah's arms.

The peculiarly sunny destiny of this woman for whom everything seemed to work out right, who had entered, and left unscathed the harem of Pharaoh, retained, in a polygamous age her husband's exclusive love, defied, by her motherhood, the laws of nature and escaped bereavement by a miracle, persisted even after her death, so that in circumstances where it might easily have been otherwise, she was buried with dignity and decorum.

By that time Abraham's wanderings had brought him into Canaan; he had just arrived in Kirjath-arba, and the land belonged to the children of Heth and he had no friend there. Nor was there a single field which he could call his own and in which he might lay his head to rest. But when Sarah was dead and the grief-stricken Abraham appealed to the people for a piece of ground as a burial place, they said—as though they knew that no ordinary woman lay there in the shrouds—"In the choice of our sepulchres bury thy dead." The answer would have pleased, but it would not have surprised Sarah, could she have known of it. She was accustomed to having ordinary rules twisted in her favour; and she would have appreciated the fact that Abraham's grief was so profound that even the children of

Heth—whose descendants were to fight so bitterly with his over this same ground—were awed by it.

So Sarah was buried in the field of Ephron, where, some years later, her granddaughter-in-law, Leah, whose story was so different, was to come to lie beside her.

But that was not the end. For Ishmael lived and became a hunter in the desert and in due time Hagar who, through all her slavery, had remained Egyptian at heart, chose him an Egyptian woman to be his wife. And if it is true, as they say it is, that he fathered the Arabs, one might reflect, not too fancifully, that the bitter strife in Palestine at this moment has its real roots, its far roots, in the inability of two women to share one roof and one man; Abraham and Ishmael and Isaac could have lived and laughed and hunted together. Hagar was powerless and supine. It was Sarah who said, "The son of the bondwoman shall not be heir with my son."

Barbed wire and bombs in Jerusalem; do they stem from, do they stir, the dust that sleeps in the field of Ephron? Do Sarah and Hagar still war, and wound one another with weapons of which they never dreamed?

Chapter 3

REBEKAH

AUTHORIZED VERSION: *Genesis 27*

"So the evil mommets do His will as well as the good, since they act the part set for them. How would it be if the play came to the hour when the villainous man must do evilly, and see! he is on his knee-bones at his prayers. Then the play would be in very poor case." (*Mary Webb*: PRECIOUS BANE)

The really dramatic, the historic moment of Rebekah's life did not arrive until she had reached middle age and was the mother of two grown men. But the story of her marriage to Isaac is interesting, both as an example of how marriages were made in the patriarchal days, and because it gives us, in the girl Rebekah, a hint of the woman she was to become.

Abraham was an old man when Isaac was born and he was a very old man by the time the boy was of marriageable age. So, because he wanted his son to marry a woman of his own people and not one of the Canaanite women amongst whom he was living, and because he was himself too old to undertake the journey, Abraham entrusted the selection of the girl and the making of the contract to a servant—who may easily have been that Eliezer to whom, in his sonless days, he had contemplated leaving all his wealth.

He gave him no special instructions to guide him—the angel of the Lord would do that, Abraham said; somehow, by some means, one special girl should be singled out and then the servant was to ask for her hand in marriage to his master's son. If she refused to leave her own people and journey off to a strange land to marry a man whom she had never seen, that would be a sign that she was not the chosen one.

So the servant, well furnished with camels and with jewels in his pouch, set off for Mesopotamia, and outside the city of Nahor he made one of those odd little bargains with himself which everyone makes from time to time. There would be many young marriageable girls in Nahor, how should he know which one to choose? He would choose the one—if one there were—who offered him and his camels water—a girl, in short, of friendly, hospitable disposition; and no idler, since water for a man and ten thirsty camels would take some drawing.

As soon as the servant had settled upon this prearranged sign, Rebekah, who was Abraham's niece, emerged with her jug to draw water; and the servant made his request of her, and she gave him water to drink and then offered to draw water for his camels. So the servant opened his pouch and gave her a golden earring which weighed half a shekel, and two bracelets for her hands, ten shekels' weight. And he asked her her name and her father's name and whether there would be room in her father's house for him to lodge. Rebekah told him her name and added, "We have both straw and provender enough, and room to lodge in." Then the servant felt that the sign had been given him, and he bowed down and worshipped the Lord.

Rebekah ran home to make ready for the unexpected guest, and showed off her jewels and told how she had acquired them, and her brother Laban (who was to cheat her son and to be cheated by him) went out to welcome the stranger; and within the house a feast was prepared. But the servant was faithful. Before he partook of food he explained all his errand and told them how great and rich Abraham had become in the new country, and how he had but one son who was to inherit all his property and how it was essential that he should marry within the family, and how he had arranged the sign by which he should know the chosen woman, and how Rebekah had behaved exactly in the way he had decided to accept as a touchstone. Then there was great excitement in the house; increased, when the servant produced more jewels, and ornaments of silver and gold, and presents for Laban and for Rebekah's mother—all the things the ten swaying camels had carried out of Canaan. The feast lasted well into the night; but in the morning the faithful servant was active and ready, eager to get back to Abraham and tell again the exciting, dramatic story of his wonderful good luck, or good guidance.

But Rebekah's mother and brother pled for a little delay, ten days at least. The text reads as though they had made all these neat arrangements without consulting the person most concerned, and this plea for delay hints at the idea that they were not absolutely sure of Rebekah's reaction; they needed, one feels, at least ten days in which to accustom her to the plan and to persuade her. However, when the servant insisted upon returning at once, they said they would ask the girl herself, and they called her in and said, "Wilt thou go with this man?" The servant held his breath—for that question and its answer had been imagined by Abraham. And Rebekah said, "I will do." No delay, no hesitation, no doubt, no conditions. Not merely a generous, hospitable girl, but an adventurer, an acceptor of life—a good wife for a boy who, although he had great possessions, was a stranger in a strange land, an exile, a sojourner.

She left her home as a girl of good family should, with the blessing of her relatives ringing in her ears and with her nurse and her damsels riding behind her. And days later, in the cool of the evening, Isaac "went out to meditate in the field," meditating no doubt about the appearance and the nature of the woman who had been chosen for him in this arbitrary fashion, and lifted his eyes and saw the camel train approaching. At the same time Rebekah turned to the servant and asked, "What man is this that walked in the field?" And the servant told her that it was Isaac; so she took a veil and covered herself, the age-old gesture of the bride. And all was well, Isaac loved her, "and was comforted after his mother's death" by his wife. The skilful inclusion of those few words suggests that he was young and that he transferred, from the dominant, possessive Sarah, something of adoration, something of dependence, towards Rebekah who was well able to accept it. The girl who could ride away with a servant into an unknown country, to meet an unknown bridegroom without one fear or doubt or question was a worthy successor to Sarah.

The years passed. Rebekah, like Sarah, was barren for a time, and then she bore twin sons. Before their birth, she—like Sarah and like Hagar, received the promise of God that her children should be the founders of nations; but to the promise there was added the unusual prophecy that the elder should serve the younger. Rebekah laid that prophecy away in her heart, storing it—if Biblical time is accurate—for forty years.

The children were called Esau and Jacob. They were not identical twins; they were in fact very different. Esau was hairy, Jacob smooth. Esau was a hunter, a wild man, a reversal to an older type; Jacob was "a plain man, dwelling in tents," in fact a man of the new kind, pastoral, agricultural, the emergent pattern, the type upon which Israel was to be reared. Isaac loved Esau. One rather regrets the reason given in the Bible, but there it is, not to be controverted, "Isaac loved Esau because he did eat of his venison." But the sentence could be symbolic. Isaac, the meek, the law-abider, weighed down by the destiny laid upon him by his father's ideology, dominated first by his mother and then by his wife, probably saw in Esau the essence of an old, lost freedom. Esau did not tend flocks or till fields, he hunted when he was hungry and rested when he was full-bellied. Esau belonged to the past. Even his hairiness speaks of a time when men had no need for donned raiment; Esau stands, I think, for the primitive, the thing which was being left behind.

And it was left for Rebekah to see that, and to understand.

So we come to the moment when an old blind man sits at the doorway of a tent and feels the weight of his years, and thinks about death and about the thing which he must do before he can die in peace. As he sees it, he is priest as well as patriarch, and has a solemn rite to perform, the choosing and blessing of his successor. And he calls for his first-born son, Esau the hunter.

But Rebekah is watching and listening. She herself is no longer young, but compared with Isaac her husband she is vigorous and vital, and has, at this moment, strength outside her own to call upon. For more than forty years she has watched and waited for this moment when she must seize the thread of a seemingly smooth-spun destiny, twist it out of line, knot it and secure it forever. She thinks—and thousands of people lightly scanning her story think with her—that she is acting out of a maternal partiality for her younger son. Actually she is merely Jehovah's tool. She takes advantage of an old blind man, but was it not for this moment that he was made blind?

The thing which Isaac had to give to his son was an imponderable. It is called sometimes a "blessing," sometimes a "birthright," and it had its roots far back in Jehovah's selection of Abraham as a repository of the new idea of Godhead. In return for faith, for a confidence in the unseen and the unproven, and for a willingness to be isolated from his fellow men, Abraham received a blessing and a promise which passed on to his son Isaac and was now about to be passed on to Esau. But Esau, although the physical descendant, the legitimate elder son, was not the spiritual heir of his father or his grandfather. Esau had already shown that by marrying two Hittite women, Judith and Bashemath, an action which brought "grief of mind unto Isaac and to Rebekah." Esau was not Jehovah's man; Jacob, despite all his twists and shifts and guilefulness, was. Yet Isaac, because of his personal preference or because of a conventional respect for primogeniture was going to "bless" Esau, to appoint him as his spiritual as well as his material heir, and vest the mysterious birthright in him.

So he sent Esau out to kill a deer and to dress it and prepare him his favourite dish which he would eat in a sacrificial sense. And while Esau was out on his hunting Rebekah acted. She probably did not understand what she was doing or why she was doing it. It is unlikely that she really saw clearly and spiritually enough to see that Jacob was the better tool for the rearing of one more step in the long path of man's approach to God; what she did know and what she did understand was that Esau was about to be shown some favour, given some advantage which she coveted for her favourite son. So she sent Jacob out to kill two kids from the flock and said that she would dress them and that he should carry in the savoury dish and receive the blessing.

Jacob protested—not out of his scruples but out of fear. He knew that the blind man depended upon his sense of touch and said, "Behold. Esau my brother is a hairy man, and I am a smooth man; my father peradventure will feel me and I shall seem to him as a deceiver; and I shall bring a curse upon me and not a blessing." Then the girl who had dared the long journey and the unseen bridegroom spoke from the mouth of the middle-aged woman, "Upon me be thy curse, my son; only obey my voice. . . . " And Jacob obeyed her. So she made the flavoursome dish, and then she took the soft silky pelts of the young kids and fitted pieces of them across the smooth hands and smooth neck of the pretender. And since in the blind man another sense was sharpened, she took away Jacob's clothes which smelt of sheep and the tent's smoky fires and cooking meals and made him wear the clothes of Esau, redolent of the woods and the fields and the earth.

Then she had done all she could and must wait, her hands clenched with anxiety, her pulses bounding with excitement, for the moment when Jacob should come out and say that all was well.

Perhaps as she waited she looked at the gold bracelets upon her wrists and reached up to finger the heavy gold earring, remembering the day when they had been given her, remembering all the excitement, the sense of adventure with which she had accepted her unusual destiny. And perhaps she realised, dimly, that it had all been leading towards this day when, through her determination and resource, Jacob was to receive the blessing and the charge. They were Jacob's children who were to be as the sands of the seashore for number, as the stars of heaven for glory; it was Jacob who was to be the father of the Chosen People.

Had she any idea what it meant? Any mystic foresight of the thousands who were to call themselves Israelites and bear in their minds and their bodies the mark of their breed? Did she dream of Jerusalem in its glory, of the Babylonian captivity, the Messianic dreams, the last dispersal, the pogroms, the Ghettos? Not she. There was something of value to be given away and she wanted it for the son she loved. She did not know, nor would she much have cared, that out of that simple, feminine motive, she had committed an historic action. For the blessing and the birthright conferred upon Esau would quickly, in one generation, have vanished into the mists of superstition and idolatry and the idea of a spiritual deity might have eluded mankind for another thousand thousand years. With Jacob it was safe; he lied and he cheated, but he never lost his awareness of something behind the material aspect of the world; he believed in the existence of things that could not be seen or tasted or handled. And already, though neither he nor Rebekah knew it, his feet were set on the path that was to lead towards the dream of Bethel and the wrestling match at Peniel.

He was a little shaken when he came back to his mother, for Isaac's suspicions had not been easily lulled. The delicate, tremulous old hands of the blind man had been stretched out to touch his son—and they had been deceived. The ear had been surer. "The voice is Jacob's voice, but the hands are the hands of Esau." And then he had smelled him and been assured. And then, very solemnly, he had given him the blessing, grave enough, comprehensive enough, to have stirred a man far less sensitive than Jacob was. "Let people serve thee and nations bow down to thee; be lord over thy brethren and let thy mother's sons bow down to thee; cursed be every one that curseth thee and blessed be he that blesseth thee."

And it was not only Jacob who believed that such a blessing was potent and vital and irrevocable. Esau, when he came in from his hunting, and heard what his father had done "cried with a great and exceeding bitter cry." And Isaac, knowing himself to have been duped, knowing too that such solemn words could not be retracted, "trembled very exceedingly." He then contrived to lay a makeshift, a very second-rate blessing upon Esau who was, naturally, greatly enraged against Jacob.

But the feeling between the old man and his elder son was reciprocal; Esau said openly that he would take no vengeance upon

Chapter 4

LEAH AND RACHEL

AUTHORIZED VERSION: *Genesis 29-33*

> *"These are not flowers. They are Jacob waiting*
> *for Rachel seven years, and, when she came,*
> *Finding that April had been hesitating*
> *for seven years to justify her name."*
> (*Humbert Wolfe*: REQUIEM)

The story of Leah and Rachel falls into the same triangular pattern as that of Sarah and Hagar; two women and one man spending their lives in physical proximity and emotional conflict. In its way it is as harsh a story. It lacks the element of bondage, of the domination of one woman over the other, but to offset this mitigation there is the fact that the two women were sisters; and that the man for whose favours they were perpetually competing was less tactful, less kind-hearted than the man who was torn this way and that between Sarah and Hagar.

Rachel, the younger and more beautiful sister, figures in that delectable thing, love at first sight, and the relationship between her and Jacob appears to have been one of sustained devotion. She was the woman whom he wanted to marry; she remained his favourite wife even through the long period when she was barren; and when she bore children they were his favourites and he showed his favouritism in no uncertain fashion.

But that makes a dull story of the kind of happiness that has no history, and so, all through this three-cornered drama the perceptive eye is focussed upon Leah, the vulnerable, pitiable victim of a desperate frustration.

Writers who denigrate the Old Testament should study up on one single verse in the twenty-ninth chapter of Genesis—the verse which introduces these two women. Verse twenty-eight gives us their names and tells us that Leah was the elder. Then verse twenty-nine:—"Leah was tender-eyed; but Rachel was beautiful and well-favoured." No verse ever written surpasses that for subtlety, for compression, for significance. It tells us all about Leah, a gentle, sentimental, not very attractive woman with one good feature; and then there is the "but" sounding like a herald's note to announce an arrival that cancels all that has gone before; and "beautiful and well-favoured" conjures up the vision of young Oriental beauty, the smooth skin, the lustrous eyes, the glossy downpour of hair, the neck like a pillar, the full deep breast, and the slumbrous confidence bred of long acknowledged loveliness. No writer has done more in nine words.

They were the daughters of Laban, a prosperous sheep farmer in Padan-aram, who was the brother of Rebekah, Jacob's mother; and when Rebekah and Jacob had between them successfully hoaxed Isaac, the doting mother suggested that her son should go on a prolonged visit to his uncle, in order to be out of reach of his infuriated brother and in order to find for himself a wife within the family circle.

Whether, prior to his arrival, there had been jealousy between the two sisters, or whether they had lived in amity, the one accepting the other's beauty as a matter of course, is not told; but from the moment when he came into Padan-aram in search of hospitality and a wife, they were forced into rivalry.

All the evidence within the story points to Leah having been in love with Jacob from the beginning. Either there was something about him which does not emerge clearly, or else changing standards of behaviour prejudice our view; for even allowing for Jacob's importance as a religious instrument, there is something about his shifts and dodges, his trickiness and deceitfulness, which repels. Certainly his mother doted upon him, and Leah loved him in the face of considerable discouragement; Rachel accepted him—and she, being beautiful and young, would hardly lack suitors; and even his uncle, Laban, tolerated him for a long time.

self for the whole of that wedding night; and that night saw the death of all hope of supplanting Rachel in his heart.

For the plot failed. The morning of humiliation dawned and before the day it brought had ended Jacob had struck a new bargain with his uncle. If he could have Rachel at once he would serve for another seven years. Laban agreed to that; from his point of view it was a good bargain (though later he saw its disadvantages), but he did attempt to snatch one tiny concession for Leah. He was her father and perhaps his undazzled eyes perceived her quality, and it is pleasant to reflect that even his worldly, calculating mind was capable of entertaining an imaginative pity for the shame which she must be feeling. Jacob demanded Rachel at once, and considering those seven years of labour which had been rewarded by a gross deception, he was within his rights; but Laban argued that Leah had a right to at least a week's unrivalled attention from her husband.

But the miracle which could not be worked in a night could not be worked in a week, and those seven days must have been amongst the most miserable of all Leah's life of days. She had her husband's body—for those were simple times and simple people—but she must have known that his mind was reaching forward to Rachel's bridal bed. And at the end of the week the second marriage was celebrated; and although Leah was Jacob's wife, his first wife, taking formal precedence over her sister, after that her tent—and her bed—were lonely.

There is nowhere in the story a sign of any real hostility between the two women; or any evidence that Rachel flaunted her triumph as Hagar flaunted hers. It may be that in youth she had formed a habit of attitude towards Leah, pitying her because of her unattractiveness, and because of her vulnerability of feeling. If that were so, such pity would be enforced now when she saw her sister in the grip of an infatuation such as she herself had never known and was incapable of knowing. But although no actual quarrel is recorded, and although the only reproachful words between them fell from Leah's lips—a mild, ineffectual reproach too, typical of the woman who uttered it—there did exist for many years a most curious form of rivalry between them.

It was a kind of chess game in which the pieces were four female bodies, Leah's and her maid Zilpah's, Rachel's and her maid Bilhah's; and each success was scored in the body of a little male child who was to found, and name, one of the tribes of Israel.

Leah proved—and this too is in keeping with her type—to be easily pregnable. She bore to Jacob, in rapid succession, four male children; and with each birth, not without reason, since in the East sons are precious and the women who bear them honoured, she hoped that Jacob's feelings towards her would warm and soften. And each birth was a triumph over the beautiful favoured Rachel, who had as yet borne no child at all. But Rachel, like her husband's grandmother, Sarah, retained, despite her barrenness, her husband's affection; and it may have been through thinking over the story of Sarah and comparing her case with her own, that she conceived the idea of offering to Jacob her handmaid, Bilhah, whose son would legally count as hers. Bilhah did bear a son, and Rachel claimed him, just as Sarah had claimed Ishmael, and when he was born Rachel rejoiced and named him Dan and said, "God hath given me a son."

But Laban had treated his daughters fairly, and Leah also had her bondmaid. If one woman could have sons by proxy, so could the other. So Zilpah was offered to Jacob, and she, too, conceived and bore Gad who was naturally numbered with Leah's sons. Jacob was now the father of seven boys, and at Gad's birth Leah voiced a remark which shows that whatever she lacked she did not lack humour; she said "A troop cometh." And certainly, for any man entrusted with the task of founding a new nation, no more felicitous set of circumstances could have been devised than these which resulted in a not unamiable fertility competition. Was it by accident or design that this triangular pattern fell?

Leah's eldest son, Reuben, had reached an age when he was able to go out into the fields alone and still Rachel had no child save her bondmaiden's, and these two apparently irrelevant facts introduce us to one of the rare instances of superstition being recognised in the Bible.

One must admit that despite the antiquity of its story, despite its association with folklore, Biblical history is singularly free of anything remotely resembling magic. If you can accept as a premise an omnipotent, omniscient, yet oddly human God who communicated direct with certain men in a manner now unknown, there is very little else in the Old Testament at which reason and credulity need boggle. The story of En-dor, which deals with spiritualism, and the story of Reuben's mandrakes, which smacks of black magic, stand, I think, alone in this respect.

Young Reuben went into the field and returned, not with a handful of useful gleanings or a bunch of poppies, but with some mandrake roots, those debatable growths which some authorities deny exist at all and others identify with the common white bryony. Legend, with its origin lost in the mists of time, says that the mandrake is half human, in shape almost wholly human, unflatteringly bi-furcated. When it is pulled from the ground it shrieks with a human voice, and with its aid a barren woman may bear a child. The legend was old in Rachel's day.

Rachel, the much loved, barren wife, saw the son of her unloved but fruitful sister come in from the field with his childish treasure; she followed him into Leah's tent and struck a bargain which tells us a good deal about the triangular situation. If Leah would take some of those mandrakes out of Reuben's little hot hand and give them to her, Rachel said, Jacob should be hers for the night. It is implicit that Jacob belonged to Rachel, that he was hers to dispose of; and it is equally plain that Leah was, so far as love was concerned, a beggar, making do with crumbs.

Leah was both humiliated and frightened. She believed the story of the power of the mandrakes. If she let Rachel have them, and Rachel did conceive, her one advantage over her sister would be cancelled out. But the price was tempting—one more night with the man she loved; the chance of one more son; food indeed for a starved and insatiable love. Once before she had gambled her whole future for a night with Jacob. . . .

It was then, while the bargain was being struck that Leah spoke the only bitter words in the whole story. "Is it a small matter," she asked, "that thou hast taken my husband? And wouldest thou take away my son's mandrakes also?" That old trick, almost forgotten now, which Laban had played, entitled her to say that. Jacob had been Leah's husband first; by this time she probably believed, because she wanted to believe, that Rachel had supplanted her.

But she struck the bargain, and lest there should be any mistake about it, she met Jacob that evening as he came in from the field, and took him to her tent.

The mandrakes are not mentioned again. But presently Rachel bore her son, Joseph, whom Jacob was to love more than any of his sons, to whom he was to show the favouritism which ended in the Egyptian bondage. And it is strange to realise that Reuben, who as a little boy had come in with his magical roots, should be the one of Jacob's sons who was most susceptible to Joseph the Dreamer.

Outside this family circle which was being so rapidly augmented, things had not been going well. Jacob had been cheating Laban and Laban had been defrauding Jacob, and although the balance between the two shrewd, self-seeking men had held for a time it tipped at last, and then Jacob dreamed one of his timely dreams. In it he was ordered to return to Canaan. So while Laban was at his sheep-shearing Jacob gathered together his wives and his handmaidens and all his sons, his flocks and his herds and his serving men and set out on the long journey.

It was twenty years since he had fled to Padan-aram, but as he approached his own country he became uneasy, fearing that even the long lapse of time might not have reconciled Esau to the loss of his father's blessing, and that he might attempt some revenge. So just before he entered Canaan Jacob did two things, both extremely typical and revealing.

First he selected from his vast swarm of animals a number of sheep, goats, camels, cattle and horses, and divided them into three droves which he sent on ahead of his own caravan under the care of drovers who had orders to present the gift to Esau as soon as he should accost them. In all there were five hundred and eighty animals—an acceptable present. But the noteworthy thing is that in the preparation of this bribe Jacob betrayed himself. The mystical and imponderable blessing which he and his mother had coveted so hotly that in order to obtain it they had cheated an old blind man and wronged a young one, was thus weighed and measured, accorded its exact material value—five hundred and eighty head of stock.

Secondly—in case the present failed to appease the vengeful Esau, Jacob arranged his family in a significant marching order. And whoever else missed its significance Leah, one feels, would not. First of all rode the two handmaidens, Zilpah and Bilhah, with their children. They would take the first brunt of any unpleasantness which might arise. They were the least valuable of Jacob's women, the least cherished of his children. And after them rode Leah and her sons; all those sons, each born in hope. At the rear, under Jacob's own protection rode the favourite wife and the favourite son, Joseph. The order of march recorded wordlessly the whole of Leah's sorry history, midway between the bond slaves and the wife, that was her place. And in that place, accepted with resignation, or with bitterness, she moves out of the story.

Rachel, the beautiful and beloved, died giving birth to Benjamin and was buried at Bethlehem where Jacob reared a memorial pillar so that the place was always known as Rachel's Grave. And there is no indication in the story that after her death Jacob's love shifted its focus and centred upon the woman who had loved him for so long a time. Rachel's children, Joseph and Benjamin, were always their father's favourites. Joseph, at least, had inherited much of her beauty and unconscious charm.

But the story ends with a curious twist. Years later, when Jacob was dying in exile in Egypt and laying his last, irrevocable commands upon his attendant sons, he bade them to bury him, not in Rachel's grave at Bethlehem, but in the field which his grandfather Abraham had purchased as a burial place for Sarah. "There," he said, "they buried Abraham and Sarah his wife; there they buried Isaac and Rebekah his wife; and there I buried Leah." Was it a sense of family, of tribal tradition that made him choose to lie there, rather than at Bethlehem with the woman whom he had loved? Or was Leah's right as the first wife thus asserted and Rachel acknowledged to be a thing apart, a romantic, unprofitable diversion from the tribal path?

The sons, sons of Zilpah and Bilhah and Rachel and Leah, saw to it that their father's last wish was carried out. So at the end Leah and Jacob lay side by side. "My heart would hear and beat, were it earth in an earthy bed. . . ." Poetic licence? Or was there, in the dust, a stirring, a sense of final triumph? Once, long ago Leah had bargained for one night of love; now the last, the longest night of all, was hers.

Chapter 5

POTIPHAR'S WIFE

AUTHORIZED VERSION: *Genesis 39*

> *"Is there no virtue in bearing down the threat*
> *of the jungle moving faintly in the blood,*
> *and the smooth velvet footsteps, and the wet*
> *muzzles of creatures, stirring in the mud . . . ?"*
> (*Humbert Wolfe*: REQUIEM)

This Egyptian woman shares with two other Biblical women, "Painted Jezebel" and "False Delilah," the distinction of having lent her name to a particular type of conduct; and as a result her story is, like theirs, known to a number of people who would find it hard to say how Rebekah differed from Rachel, or Rahab from Jael. But she also has a distinction all her own. Alone of the women of the Bible she has become associated with the comparatively modern title of "Mrs.," and the fact has great significance. A woman may still bear a child late in life and not be called "Mrs. Rebekah;" betray her country and not be "Mrs. Rahab"; interest herself in unfeminine, legal business and not be "Mrs. Deborah" or, more correctly, Mrs. Lapidoth. The modernisation of the false wife's name seems to indicate that, of all female activities, attempted adultery is the most enduring, as, judging from the literature of the world it is the most interesting.

Like the other "bad" women, Jezebel and Delilah, this woman was a member of another nation. She was an Egyptian, the wife of the captain of Pharaoh's guard. We are granted no word of illumination about her age, her appearance, her history; she emerges anonymously in the midst of the story of Joseph the

Dreamer, makes her attempt at seduction, fails, takes her spiteful revenge and disappears. But she leaves a mark upon the case-history of her sex, not only in a term of opprobrium. She can be regarded as a symbolic figure; an extreme, blatant, rather pathetically ridiculous manifestation of an emotion that most honest women would admit, in secret, to be familiar.

As the wife of an important official in ancient Egypt, Potiphar's wife would lead the luxurious, secluded life of the upper-class women of the East. She was as immune from domestic cares as Pharaoh himself; if she had children—and no children are mentioned—the care of them would be undertaken by hirelings. Social work, and sport for women, were unknown, and what education she had received would at best be two-headed, a religious-magical training on how to please the gods and a more practical if more diffused training on how to please men. This latter would continue after marriage, for where polygamy is the custom a woman does not lay aside her seductive arts with her virginity. Sexuality has survived many rivals; in these harems of the East it had no rival at all. The wife of Potiphar was one of a legion of women whose interests and pleasures and achievements, whose whole reason for existence lay in the exercise of their sexual functions.

Of the second actor in this three-cornered drama we are told almost as little. He was Joseph's master, and the captain of Pharaoh's guard. That is all. He may have been elderly; high position and age are often associated in the East; he may have been young. He may have been obese and revolting, or handsome. We have no clue, save in his wife's behaviour when she was brought into contact with someone young and comely. That his age and appearance had not been considered when the marriage was arranged can be stated with some assurance. Potiphar may have chosen and desired his wife, but she would have had no say in the matter.

The story is Joseph's; so of the third participant we have more information. He was the son of Jacob and his much-loved wife, Rachel, and according to the story magical influences had been at work upon him even at the time of his conception, for he was purchased by mandrake roots which the despised Leah's son had found and which were credited with great powers. Leah had traded them with her sister for a night with Jacob. The charm had worked and Joseph had been born to be, of all Jacob's children, the favourite and best-beloved. The mark of high destiny had been upon him from the beginning. He was one of those people whom other people find it impossible to regard with indifference; liking or loathing resulted from the first contact. Nothing between. Some of his brothers loathed him; Reuben loved him. He was "a goodly person and well-favoured," full of the confident assurance bred of his father's partiality and of his own inward sense of greatness. Torn from his native desert and sold into slavery in Egypt he quickly made his mark upon the household of Potiphar. He became a favourite there, a trusted, valued steward. A slave still, but a slave with authority and a wide scope for the exercising of his administrative talent. Soon, only two years later, he was to be ruling Egypt, second only to the idle, inefficient Pharaoh, but for the moment all his dynamic energy, his quick wit, subtle intelligence and spiritual integrity were at the service of Potiphar and his household. Josephus—in this instance more generous than the Old Testament recorder—troubles to mention that Potiphar's wife fell in love with her husband's slave "both on account of his beauty of body and his dexterous management of affairs." The term "fell in love" and the suggestion of some intellectual appreciation of the boy's character at work in the woman softens, a little, the sordidness of the story. The fact that the Biblical account omits them and attributes her behaviour entirely to lust need not be taken as evidence against her; it was not her story, her motive was unimportant to the historian intent only upon recounting the effect of her behaviour upon his chief character. But in considering the case of "Mrs. Potiphar" it should be borne in mind that women are, on the whole, less completely physical in their sexual reactions than men, partly because their aesthetic responses are less sharp and overwhelming, partly because by selection and training they have, from time immemorial, been bred to regard male beauty as a thing of secondary importance. Even in these days of freedom, the woman who chooses a man solely for physical reasons is a rarity; some mental impulse, if it be only a mercenary one is usually at work. So without undue sentimentality we may grant Potiphar's wife the small extenuation which Josephus suggests.

The boy arrived, straight from the nomad life of the desert, into this sophisticated household of women, eunuchs and cringing slaves, full, as all large establishments were, of intrigue and chicanery, of nepotism and sycophancy. He was a slave. He had stood with other slaves in the marketplace, and had changed hands, like a dumb beast, upon the passing of some pieces of silver. It was an experience which would have marked an ordinary free-born desert boy for life, rendering him either miserably docile or savagely intractable, according to his nature. But for Joseph, with his unquestioning belief in his God and his dreams, the experience lacked all bitterness, it was an intrinsic part of his life plan. So he would stand out from amongst the other slaves not only by reason of his physical beauty but on account of his unmarred psychological condition as well. The wife of Potiphar probably saw him first when he was waiting upon her table, a duty which demanded an unblemished appearance; and there he moved with the grace, the calm, the detachment with which, in days so recent, he had tended his father's sheep. For him an interlude, an experience, a step upon the road which led to dreams' fulfilment. She would notice and ask his name, his place of origin. Potiphar would tell her—a Hebrew, from Canaan; and he would mention the price he had paid for so handsome a slave, congratulating himself upon a good bargain.

But the days of waiting at table and performing menial tasks were short and soon past. Potiphar, captain of Pharaoh's guard, would be a good judge of a man's worth and capacity, used to relegating duties according to ability and before long he had promoted Joseph to be his overseer and, finding him shrewd, industrious and honest, trusted him with everything in his household. His trust in the Hebrew boy was so utterly complete that, in the inimicable Bible phrase, "he knew not ought he had, save the bread which he did eat."

Joseph's promotion was watched avidly from an unsuspected

quarter. If the first sight of the handsome slave with the unslave-like bearing had waked a passing "lust of the eye," secretly shaming because evoked by a menial, it could now be justified and rationalised. Sexual selectiveness invariably demands that the object of its attention should *seem* unique, and it was all too easy for the wife of Potiphar to see in this young man such qualities as would make small the difference in their stations and justify her affection. Brooding through the long idle days, allowing her imagination full rein, she became obsessed with a desire that grew and grew until it was ungovernable.

She was forced to make the first advances. If Joseph himself had burned with a consuming passion for his mistress he could have given no sign. In her presence he was forced, by etiquette and custom, to be as sexless as an attendant eunuch, less assertive than the little dog which lay at the hem of her skirt, for the palace life in the East managed to combine the closest intimacy of service with the most rigid discipline of behaviour so that the slave who must, in the course of his duties, be familiar with her very bedchamber, might, at the same time, not even know the colour of her eyes or the form of her headdress.

Such intimacy and such remoteness could become a subtle form of torment; and if it had been Joseph who had fallen in love with his mistress the hearts of all the romantics through the ages would have bled for him. For his mistress there is never anything but scorn and ridicule, and moral condemnation. Jehovah and Jacob, Reuben and Potiphar and in time Pharaoh might love Joseph; but not this woman, although the custom of her day allowed her husband wives and concubines without number.

She was sure, beyond all shadow of doubt, that nothing but their differences in station stood between them; and one day she moved to cast all such barriers aside. One day, when they were alone in the house she, the wife of Potiphar, captain of Pharaoh's guard, one of the greatest ladies in the whole great land of Egypt, stretched out her hand to the Hebrew slave and offered to make him not only her equal but her master.

For a slave who bore even the slightest trace of resentment at his servitude, for the free-born man who had felt, even for one moment, the chafe of the yoke it was an unparalleled chance of retaliation. The measure of the temptation which Joseph withstood on this single occasion demands a full-stretched imagination for its understanding. The saints, we read, have at times been tempted by the vision of lovely, amorous women; for Odysseus there was the song of the sirens; but these were one-dimensional, fleshly lures. No inner, secret sense of achievement and self-aggrandisement could have been reached by succumbing to the temptation. This young slave could by a single action have made cuckold the man who had estimated his bodily worth in terms of petty cash, could have taken possession of the object dearest to Potiphar's pride if not his heart. Even if the woman were not overwhelmingly attractive in person the circumstances surrounding her offer made it peculiarly tantalising to a lonely, inexperienced young man, cut off from normal female society and thrust, through no fault of his own, into a menial position.

Potiphar's wife reclined upon her cushions and the young slave, summoned to her apartment, stood by her couch. Every skill which art had devised and an age-old inheritance of knowledge had passed down would have gone to her beautification, sweet ointments for the skin, oil and henna for the hair, silken robes that veiled and yet revealed, sweet aphrodistic perfumes scattered. She offered it all to the grave-faced, brown desert boy in his plain white slave's clothing—reaching across the gulf, stooping, supplicant.

But there was so much of Joseph of which she knew nothing. She saw a body provocative of desire, a character that induced respect. The spirit, unevidenced, unguessed at, was hidden. What could she know of his dreams? Once through a long night he had stood erect while the sun and the moon and eleven stars had made obeisance to him. What was one woman's fall compared with the bowing of the sun? His flesh might respond now to the fleshly call, his mind might seethe with triumph and pride, with wonder, speculation; but his soul, like his sheaf in that other dream, stood upright, untouched, untouchable. That pale, scented suppliant hand might flatter the slave, rouse the man, but it could never reach the dreamer who had had the stars at his feet. For he was convinced that the dreams were of God, this strange, new, often puzzling God who was at once an intangible spiritual concept and a pattern of behaviour. Jehovah had not yet thundered from Sinai, "Thou shalt not commit adultery," but the edict was formed, waiting in the womb of time. This tempted slave's descendants were to receive it, graved in stone, but for him it was graved already, implicit both in the understanding that his master trusted him completely and in the belief that when his God intended him to take a woman it would be possible for him to do so in honour, without any breach of integrity.

So he resisted his tempter; gently; firmly; giving his reason in terms that she could understand, if she chose to do so. But there was no understanding in her. Within the strict limits laid down by convention and custom she had been used to having her own way, to possessing the thing that took her fancy. He was shy, she thought, diffident, ridiculously squeamish. She tried again and again, until the day came when they were alone in the house and the scented white hand, no longer trusting to the appealing gesture, closed upon the slave's garment; if she could drag him to her, if flesh touched warm flesh there would be no more hesitation.

This time he did not stay to explain or to excuse himself. Panic-stricken, fleeing, perhaps from the woman, perhaps from the temptation itself, he wrenched himself away, leaving part of the loose linen robe in her hand.

It may have been lust diverted into venom or it may have been fear that prompted her next, inexcusable action. The text actually suggests that fear played a part, for it reads, "when she saw that he had left his garment in her hand . . . that she called . . ." The garment was evidence against her, difficult to dispose of, impossible to explain save in the one way which she chose. She had no time for reflection or for subtlety. Before Joseph, the trusted, dignified steward, could be seen, flustered and half naked, running from her apartments she had screamed and was telling the story which would explain the whole situation. The slave had attempted to rape her and upon her outraged cry had fled, leaving his discarded robe behind him.

Potiphar believed her. Experience had taught him that all men had some weakness and it would be easy to believe that the slave who had seemed almost too perfect was, after all, flawed like other men. If the story reached the supper tables of the nobility of Egypt it led to wise pronouncements upon the superiority of eunuchs as harem attendants and upon the dubiousness of good bargains. Perhaps some of the women who had visited Potiphar's house and seen Joseph wondered and smiled.

The name "Joseph" has, like that of his tempter, been used to denote a certain form of behaviour and often with a slightly derogatory flavour; but it is noteworthy that he allowed himself to be disgraced, seemingly hopelessly, and thrust into prison without uttering a single word in his own defence. Such complete and shining chivalry is not to be dismissed by the suggestion that defence was hopeless. He could have sown a seed of doubt in Potiphar's mind which would have lived to bear many petty bitter fruits. That much of revenge was his for the taking; but he went to his dungeon in silence. The slave market, the palace, the prison were all the same to him, steps upon the predestined road. Small wonder that so unique a prisoner was soon finding favour in the sight of the keeper of the prison.

Did "Mrs. Potiphar" wake in the night and turn from erotic dream to remorseful thoughts of airless confinement, meagre rations, lice and fever and rats; or was her torment confined to her own wounded vanity? Did she search her mirror, or her heart, or the face of her husband? The story gives no clue. It sweeps on to the story of Joseph's triumph, the vindication that is familiar in every Sunday school. Nobody wonders what conflicting, tumultuous emotions a clean white linen garment could ever afterwards rouse in this woman's mind. Her part had been played; a mean, slightly ridiculous figure, she passes from the stage.

But at the other end of the Bible there is a sentence which is not irrelevant to the story of Potiphar's wife. Christ said a shrewd thing about lustful looking being the equivalent of adultery. He spoke of men but the dictum applies equally to the women who judge Potiphar's wife. How much of their popularity, one wonders, do the stars of stage and screen owe to this same "lustful looking"? Should we, like Potiphar's wife, search our mirror, or our heart?

Chapter 6

RAHAB

AUTHORIZED VERSION: *Joshua 2:1-24; 6:25*

If there had survived, from the sack of Jericho, one Canaanitish historian who was subsequently inspired to write his version of the city's fall, the name of Rahab would have figured very blackly therein, and might have become a synonym for treachery. But Rahab's history has come down to us in the chronicles of Israel whose cause she adopted and whose spies she sheltered and so this Canaanitish woman who helped to betray her city to the enemy is presented to us as a Biblical heroine, recognised not only in the Old Testament but also in the New, where, twice at least, she is favourably mentioned. In history, as in war, there are some strange shiftings of standards.

Rahab's story is set in a very critical, and therefore interesting, period of Israel's history. A phase had ended. Moses, who had brought the tribes up from the Captivity in Egypt, had lived just long enough to stand upon the eminence of Pisgah and see with his earthly eyes the country so familiar to his spiritual sight. The Exodus was over, and with it the leadership of the wise, sorely tried, old man. Now was the time for conquest; and, as though symbolically, the reins of governance fell from the hands of a diplomat and a saint into those of a soldier. Joshua had been chosen to drive out the Canaanites and establish the twelve tribes in the land which God had promised to Abraham, their forefather.

That was a legend which had never died through all the years of slavery in Egypt, all the years of wandering in the wilderness; and it was not as intruders or invaders that they looked down at last upon the fruitful valley of the Jordan river. They were coming home. There lay the land in which, before he died, Abraham had finally established himself, where Isaac, his son, had lived and begotten Jacob who in turn had reared his twelve sons. Famine had driven them out of their inheritance and the years of exile had been long, but they had come back, not a mere family, but twelve strong tribes with the making of a nation within them, ready to take possession.

From their hiding places in the mountains the Hebrews looked down upon the Jordan valley and saw it as the dream-come-true of land-hungry men fresh from the desert. Spies had crept down and come back with mouth-watering tales of its luxuriant fertility; but those tales, and the more tangible proofs which the spies carried back, had another, darker significance. Those grapes which swung so heavily between the poles of the spies had been planted and tended by men who would not easily abandon the soil over which they had sweated; the milk and honey with which the land was flowing told of a settled, agricultural people who would take arms to guard their rights. This was no unpopulated island, no uninhabited oasis, and there at the head of the valley, a symbol of defiant guardianship stood the strong-walled city of Jericho. It had risen there as a protection against invasion from the mountains; it had repelled land-hungry raiders before and looked ready to do so again.

Joshua, looking down from the mountains, judged the walls to be twenty feet high, and sentries made their rounds along its top, so thick it was. Where the busy trade roads ended, the wall was pierced by gateways, overlooked by strong towers and fitted with gates which were closed at night, or in times of danger. It was a formidable obstacle in the Jews' path. But Joshua was less concerned with its appearance of impregnability than with its inward state. Before he moved he must know what kind of army the King of Jericho had at his command, what was the mind of the ordinary people and whether those outwardly unassailable walls had weaknesses within. To this end he sent out his spies again, and two men whose names are not even remembered stole down from the hills and entered the city.

They were not immediately noticed and suspected. The course of the story proves that they spoke a language understood in the city; their Semitic features were not remarkable in a Semitic city and, if their clothes and accents were strange, they were not alone in that, for Jericho was a busy trade centre where aliens were no novelty. But the presence of Joshua and his host in the hills was known to the people of the city, and the danger from spies was recognised; at a time when all strangers were subjected to nervous scrutiny something about Joshua's men did eventually give rise to comment and that in turn to suspicion. But before that happened the two spies had found a friend.

In both the Old Testament and the New, she is called bluntly a harlot; Josephus–not usually mealy-mouthed–says that she was an inn-keeper; other authorities have suggested that she was by trade a dyer because of the flax on her roof and the mention of the scarlet cord. But in those days of unspecialised industry there must have been flax drying on many a roof in Jericho, and a scarlet cord would be no rarity. It is possible that Rahab combined all three trades, but only the most tragic of them is a certainty. It was the motive force behind her behaviour.

The spies lodged with her, and were perhaps the first men to treat her respectfully in many years. At first, at least, as strangers, they would be unaware of the dreary trade to which the house that sheltered them and the woman who befriended them, were devoted. And later, when they knew the truth, they would not take advantage of it because they were dedicated to a mission. It is reasonable to suppose that Joshua had picked his spies carefully, choosing young men in the prime of life, with the physical fitness and keen wits which their task demanded and with the kind of manner that would be useful in an awkward situation should one arise; in this, as well as in their attitude towards her as a woman, they would make a striking contrast to Rahab's usual clientele. Those to whom the gift is denied, the callowly young, the unpalatably aging, the physically unattractive are the customers for bought love. Measuring the two young Israelites against the men she knew, the shrewd harlot would be inclined not only to regard them with favour, but to conclude that, if they were representative of the invaders, her city was doomed.

The length of time during which they "lodged" in her house is not mentioned; nor is any conversation until the last recorded; but when the spies returned to Joshua they reported verbatim Rahab's assessment of her fellow-citizens' state of mind, which rather indicates that upon other subjects they had invited her opinion and afterwards confirmed it from their own observations. And perhaps in exchange for the information she could give them they talked to her about the promise which had been made to their forefather and of the intricate and sometimes almost imperceptible stages of its fulfilment.

If she ever knew a moment of wavering indecision there is no hint of it in the story. The King of Jericho, warned of the presence of Israelite spies within his walls, sent to Rahab and demanded that she should bring them forth and instantly she had chosen her course, uttered her lie and sent her fellow-countrymen on their futile search of the river fords while the men for whom they were looking lay snugly hidden under the flax upon her roof. But that decision was not made then; an impulse however momentary it may seem is the result of influences and tendencies that reach back through the years. Rahab sheltered the spies because she had no love of her native city or of her fellow-citizens. Joshua's spies were safe in that house because the respectable people of Jericho had pointed to it with derisory fingers, looked at it with sneers. In that betrayal is indicated the whole story of the woman; there are the skirts drawn aside in the public places, the whispers, the outspoken insults; there are the men whose lust had used her and whose hypocrisy had passed her, slant-eyed, in the streets; there are the women whose scorn had stung. A lifetime of outlawry, concomitant with her profession, had denationalised Rahab. Owing loyalty to no man, how could she be loyal to a city?

Her trade served her now. It was likely enough that to such a house men might come and be asked no questions, and leave again without disclosing either their identities or their nationalities. The King's messengers were so little suspicious that they did not even wait to search the house. Why should she lie? What was one man more than another to Rahab the harlot?

They clattered away and the gates of the city were closed and barred. In the very heart of the night, when Jericho slept and only the drowsy sentries made their perfunctory rounds, Rahab climbed up to her roof with a stout rope in her hand. She roused the spies from their hiding place under the flax and conversed with them in hurried whispers. She professed her faith in their God and her belief that Joshua's host would conquer the city. Without a single plaintive, patriotic word she spoke of her country's doom. And then she dissociated herself from it and struck her bargain. A greater woman, convinced of the Israelite's victory, or sentimentally pushed into treason by her personal liking for the spies, might have been prepared to let her own chance rest upon the fortune of war; or even have been resigned to sharing the fate of her fellows. But Rahab was a trader, and a cynic. She did not trust the spies to remember her service to them. Before they left she had extracted their promise that in the event of a Hebrew victory she and her family should be spared.

When the promise was given and the sign—a scarlet cord hung from the window of the house on the wall—arranged, she let the men down, one after the other, into the darkness. Then she drew in the rope and stood for a few moments listening. There was no outcry, no sound of running feet. The spies stole away to hide in the hills until the alarm had died down and the fords of Jordan were no longer watched for their passing.

Once they were gone and the rope withdrawn, Rahab was safe. No woman in the whole of Jericho, no cherished woman in any of its palaces or mansions was so safe as Rahab in her little mud house of ill-repute on the city wall. Standing, the ramparts afford her their unquestioning shelter; breached, they but admit her friends.

Everyone knows the result of the siege of Jericho; how the priests blew on their trumpets and all the people shouted and the walls, as the Negro spiritual has it, "came tumbling down."

The scarlet thread hung in Rahab's window and was matched that day by the scarlet streams that ran in the streets, for not only was every man, woman and child in Jericho put to the sword but every sheep and ox and ass as well. Only the harlot and her family were spared. She lived to take an honoured place in Israel; legend whispered that she married Joshua.

Her memory lives in two oddly paradoxical references in the New Testament. Any man's woman while she lived, she seems to serve, after death, as a peg for any man's argument. When the superior merits of faith or works formed the subject of hot altercations she is quoted, in the Epistle to the Hebrews, as a supreme example of faith; a mere two pages on, in the Epistle of James, she is held up as an instance of the supremacy of works. But in each case she is "Rahab the harlot." The meditations and searchings of centuries leave only one thing certain about her—her profession.

Chapter 7

JEPHTHAH'S DAUGHTER

AUTHORIZED VERSION: *Judges 11*

"It is expedient that one man should die for the people."
(John 11:50)

She has no name of her own. The chronicler, hastily scribbling down the record of assaults and affrays and victories while they were fresh in his own memory or upon the tongues of his informants, included her brief and pitiable story without realising its tremendous significance. Otherwise, surely, he would have discovered her name and handed it on to us.

But he could not know what we, looking backwards know, that this young murdered girl is one of the salient landmarks in the long history of man's dealing with God. She stands, in all her young loveliness, with flowers in her hair and her timbrel in her hand, her dancing feet prematurely stilled, at the meeting place of the old and new ideologies. When her flesh charred and her veins burst and her bones calcined in the sacrificial flame it was not only the body of Jephthah's daughter which was destroyed; there too the idea of human sacrifice being acceptable to Jehovah shrivelled and was consumed. There is no record of any child, any virgin, any human being of any kind, ever being offered upon those altars again.

Her story is as brief as it is tragic. Her father, Jephthah, whose great and terrible mistake has made his name, through hers, immortal, was a stern hard man, hammered by adverse circumstances. He was the son of a harlot, but he was reared in the house of his father in company with his father's legitimate sons. They never accepted him as one of the family and when he grew to be a man of formidable physique and personality his half-brothers combined to turn him out, saying that they would not share their inheritance with him. So, a landless man, Jephthah had three alternatives from which to choose; he could have gone into the desert as a nomad, adding sheep to sheep and goat to goat; he could have hired himself out as a menial labourer; or he could become a soldier of fortune, as later, in circumstances superficially similar though fundamentally different, David did.

Jephthah chose the third alternative. He took himself into the land of Tob and there gathered about him a band of men of similar character and circumstance. The Bible speaks of them as "vain men": Josephus speaks as though they constituted a small standing army. Their method of life was probably disreputable, their swords would be for any man's hire and in slack times they would live on what they could extort, either by terrorising or by promising to protect from terrorisation, their more peaceable, more productive fellows. Not, perhaps, "good citizens," but they preserved intact a spirit of recklessness and adventure which was vanishing from Israel with every passing year as the Israelites settled down into the pastoral, agricultural pattern of settled life. In fact Jephthah lived as Hereward the Wake lived before the Norman invasion, his hand against that of every man save his immediate patron—outlawed, landless, living by his sword.

In times of peace soldiers and adventurers seldom enjoy popularity.

> "It's Tommy this, and Tommy that, and Tommy how's your soul?
> But it's thin red line of heroes when the drums begin to roll."

And presently "the drums began to roll" in Israel and Ammon. The Ammonites, another of the tribes—like the Philistines and the Amalekites—who had resisted the first invasion of the Israelites and been defeated, and retired, licking their wounds and waiting for vengeance, now returned to the fight, and the Israelites could find no leader until somebody thought of the outlawed

Jephthah, who had at least kept his sword bright. So they sent to him and asked him to be their leader in the new war.

Jephthah was then neither young, nor callow, nor soft enough to be flattered by their choice. He returned them a harsh answer and said, "If ye bring me home again to fight against the children of Ammon, shall I be your head?" At the same time he reminded them that according to their laws he had been driven out and disinherited. His answer may have given some offence, but they had no one else comparable as a leader, so they returned him a civil answer and accepted his terms. So Jephthah came back into his native Gilead, with his little band of free-booters, and busied himself in hammering an army out of men who of late had given more attention to their plough-shares than to their swords. Until recently Jephthah and his followers had been "vain men"; they had neither tilled nor reaped; but now that the well tilled, well reaped fields were in danger of invasion, their quality was recognised.

Jephthah had the weaknesses concomitant with his strength. He was bold and vigorous, but he had a materialistic mind. It must, too, be remembered that for a long time he had been living outside the radius of Jehovah's revelation. It is impossible fully to understand Jephthah's story without seeing the Israelitish idea of an invisible, unbribable, utterly different God, as a belief maintaining itself, not always without difficulty, in the midst of a surrounding darkness of superstition, nature-worship and idolatry. Deborah, when she was called upon to free Israel from an infinitely more menacing enemy, and was moreover compelled to lead her army by proxy, had the confidence of an assured and certain faith. Jephthah lacked that—and for that lack his daughter must pay. For he fell back upon the age-old practice of trying to bribe the gods. During his outlawry he had been in close touch with the older forms of religion in Canaan, and at this critical moment of his life, when he was faced with the first really important task of his career, he did, on a large scale what almost everyone has done in some degree—promised Heaven some reciprocal offering of action or behaviour in return for a specific favour.

On the eve of going into action against the Ammonites Jephthah promised Jehovah that, if He would grant him a victory, he would offer as a sacrifice the first thing that came out of his house to meet him on his return from the battle.

He must have had some actual creature in mind. He used the word "whatsoever." He was thinking, perhaps, of a favourite hound, bounding out with vociferous welcome; or a horse, allowed, Arab fashion, to wander free and knowing his master's step; or a tame deer; or something more exotic, a marmoset, peacock, or leopard cub, left at his house by some trade caravan in repayment for hospitality in a desolate place. What exactly he was thinking of when he made that vow we cannot know, but we can be sure that, whatever memory of form and colour hung at the back of his mind as he tendered his bribe, it was not, in form and colour, the young girl, excited and jubilant, who did actually come out to meet him. Did he count on the horse being fleeter of foot, the hound keener of hearing, or even some little slave boy being more assiduous to run and carry in his master's sword?

Jephthah had made his vow and struck his bargain with his God in the manner of the old times when men believed that the gods were bribable, for a good deal of the old religion still clung to the new, some of it to be absorbed and transformed, some to be sloughed off gradually and some to be amputated painfully. Jephthah's case is one of amputation.

One sees him in the hour of his triumph approaching his home. Jehovah has kept His part of the bargain and the Ammonites have been completely defeated. Jephthah whom the family and the tribe have exiled and scorned, has proved himself the saviour of Israel, and is now the acknowledged leader of the land. For him it was a heady moment, with the future opening golden before him. He comes home full of dreams and plans. Then he sees his own house and remembers his vow, and wonders which of his living possessions will first set foot upon that fateful piece of path between him and the house door. And it opens, and out steps his daughter, his only child, eager to meet her father.

She was young, not old enough for betrothal or marriage, yet old enough to have caught some glimpse of her woman's destiny and have dreamed her girlish dreams; and she was lovely with youth, with the inevitable, though, alas, so often fleeting charm that goes with early nubility. And being her father's only child gave her an importance, a standing, which, as a mere daughter in a family she could never have attained. That was inevitable too, for it was predestined that Jephthah, and through him all Israel, was to be taught a hard lesson; and callous as it may seem to say so, if this maiden had been one of several daughters, or if she had had a brother, the sacrifice which Jephthah was to make would have been easier, less dramatic, and therefore far less reaching in its result.

The young girl had heard of her father's wonderful victory, and now she came out to meet him, to dance and make music for him as Miriam danced before the Ark in the old days, and as, for centuries to come, Hebrew women were to dance and make music on joyful occasions. All the way back from the battlefield Jephthah had been met by the dances and congratulatory chanting of flower-decked, music-making women, and this ritual welcome, a miniature of the others, specially performed for him by his own young daughter, should have been most precious and sweet of all, the very crown of his triumph.

He should have been able to run to meet her, clasp her in his arms, lift her and carry her towards the house, try his hard, unskilled hand upon her timbrel and laugh when she took the flowers from her own head to place them, lop-sidedly, upon his helmet. But between him and such simple, such deserved happiness, lay the dark memory of his vow, made in a moment when he doubted not only himself, but his God. So he could only cry, broken-heartedly, "Alas, my daughter, thou hast brought me very low." Already the blood and the flame and the smoke of the sacrificial place tortured his sight. And then the thing, the "whatsoever" whom he would have been willing to hand over to such a fate would come running to meet him, and Jephthah's bitter cup brimmed.

What makes the story at once more and less tragic is the girl's unusual calibre. She accepted her fate without any kind of protest or resentment or self-pity. She saw the force of her father's vow and the inevitability of its performance. One feels that any girl capable of such devotion to Israel's cause, such complete self-immolation, should have lived and married and bred many children to inherit such qualities and be reared in such a high tradition. But her acceptance of her fate does do something to redeem the horror of it. The death of a willing martyr does differ from the death of a condemned felon even when, pain for pain, they are identical. The idea of dying for a purpose does open a window even upon the darkness of death, and because she understood and accepted what was to happen to her, Jephthah's daughter was martyr rather than victim, and at certain exalted moments during her few remaining days she could draw a courage and hope for life after death from the fact that she was paying the price of her father's victory and of Israel's freedom.

She did ask one favour, lay down one condition; that the day for the vow's fulfilment might be postponed for two months while she went, with certain female companions, into the mountains to bewail her virginity. There may here be some reference to an old Canaanitish custom otherwise lost in oblivion. Nubile young females were normally closely guarded in primitive societies; and in any case one would have thought that Jephthah—and his wife if she were living—would have wanted to share every moment of the time that remained to their daughter. But we are told that Jephthah said "Go" and that she went, with her companions, and for two months bewailed her virginity upon the mountains. It must be accepted as part of the story.

It is a situation, a two-month space, which hardly bears thinking about. There were bound to be moments of forgetfulness when tried companionship and shared youth would oust all thought of tragedy, when girlish spirits would rise, and laughter and chatter take the place of mourning, and then suddenly the realisation would fall, hard and cold as hail on a summer's day—she is doomed, she must die soon, and horribly, she has no future. Every kindness, every consideration shown her would be tainted by that thought, a tacit comment upon her apartness. Her young companions were going back to their homes, to become wives, mothers, proud and fond and honoured, old grandmothers placid in the sun with their grandchildren upon their knees. Jephthah's daughter was going by the horrible way of sacrifice into the darkness from which there was no return, about which there were many speculations, many hopes, but no certainty.

For her there must have been many moments when the impulse to self-surrender failed, when the strong self-preservative instinct that is in every living creature came uppermost, violent, clamourous. There must have been times when the sticks crackling under the pot, the savour of roast meat upon the air must have sickened her by their kinship with other fires, other flesh. Did she look at her hands, so smooth and supple, so cunningly fashioned to perform a myriad complicated actions; at her feet, so nimble and swift? Did she think of her body, so nearly ripe for love, made for love and the bearing of children; of her heart whose steady beats were numbered; of her head where thought and memory, imagination and the senses' delight conducted their indescribable mysteries within the narrow confines of the bony skull? And did she think, how could she forebear to think that no number of conquests, no amount of peace in Israel was worth—for one second—setting against the knowledge that she must die, violently, painfully, prematurely, upon an appointed day? Over and over again she must have asked herself Why, why, why?

It is so easy now to see why, or to imagine that we see why. But there was no answer to that question upon the mountains. And the days shed away like beads from a broken string and the time came for Jephthah's daughter to look her last upon the world and go to the altar.

And as she did so the dark hand of an age-old superstition reached out in Israel and attempted to drag the new, stumbling religion back to the level of the ancient ones, to set Jehovah with Baal and Moloch, with Osiris and Astaroth. For an hour, as the greasy black smoke rolled skywards Jehovah was diminished, made one with the old cruel gods, the takers of vows and bribes, into whose greedy bloody maws children and virgins had poured since time immemorial. Then, as never again until the lost days between Good Friday and Easter morning, the fate of the whole of the religious world hung in the balance.

But men like Abraham and Isaac and Jacob and Moses and Joshua and Gideon had not lived and thought in vain. Already the concept of a spiritual God to whom bribes and fantastic vows and slaughtered virgins were distasteful, was rooted in the minds of men more enlightened than the agonised Jephthah. The full horror of his vow and its result must have been the talk of Israel, and thinking men asked themselves searching questions, and the scribes began to look through the books of the law. For though no ram appeared to save this girl as Isaac was saved, though no angered voice cried from the sky, no timely deluge put out the flames, this sacrifice put into action what is undoubtedly the strongest force of any in the world—the force of public opinion. If this sacrifice were necessary, or acceptable, men argued, then how was Jehovah better than Baal? The scribes found the answer in the book of Leviticus. There was plainly set down the proof of Jehovah's mercy. He understood men and knew that in times of stress and agony men were apt to make rash vows; but because He was not Baal or Moloch He had ordered that men should be allowed to redeem such vows in the cool aftermath of passion. "A singular vow" such as Jephthah's could have been redeemed by the payment of ten shekels.

So Jephthah's daughter had not died in vain, or merely to pay for a victory over Ammon; her death and the feelings and the heart-searchings that it occasioned enabled the Hebrews—the laboratory explorers of religion—to take a great step forward toward the final truth of God as something inherent in the minds of men of goodwill, not as an exterior deity to be bribed and placated. If Jehovah would accept ten shekels instead of a human sacrifice, then human sacrifice could not be one of the things He demanded of His people.

And lest men should forget, lest another man, as ignorant and honourable as Jephthah, should look back and align Jehovah with Moloch and Baal, the young girls of Israel kept, year after year, the festival of Jephthah's daughter; four days of memorial mourning for the virgin whose blood had purchased, not merely a victory and peace for Israel, but the young religion's emancipation from the ugliest rite of the old ones.

Chapter 8

DEBORAH AND JAEL

AUTHORIZED VERSION: *Judges 4*

> *"What hand and brain went ever paired?*
> *What heart alike conceived and dared?"*
> (*Browning*: THE LAST RIDE TOGETHER)

They would not, I think, mind this linking of their names. If they ever walk in the place of shades together Jael must often look at Deborah curiously and a little enviously, wondering why their common story should have left them with such differing reputations. Deborah said, "Up!" and a thousand arrows rained from the air upon Sisera's men: Jael, all alone, without the encouragement of company, and risking her husband's wrath, drove the nail which made certain that never again would Sisera muster an army and swoop down upon Israel. Were the actions so different? Yet godly men of every persuasion, over a span of centuries, have christened their daughters Deborah, and what girl was ever named for Jael? The very mention of her name evokes from the good average person a slight shudder and the exclamation, "Oh, Jael, the woman who did something horrid with a tent nail!"

Why does it cling, this faint shadow of opprobrium, to Jael? Her motive was patriotic, her action resourceful and prompt, yet no one thinks of her as a heroine. One allows for the fact that until recently historians have been men, and that men have a preference for women as instigators rather than as participators in violent action; but it must be remembered that Jael had no one to whom she could delegate a necessary, but probably distasteful, job. One is driven to wonder whether her unpopularity does not derive from the fact that she refutes the age-old belief that no woman can drive a straight nail. Less fanciful reasons have marred many a reputation.

It is pleasant to reflect that Deborah, at least, gave her her due, and in her lifetime, and that the poem with which she celebrated Israel's victory over the Canaanites would be chanted throughout the length and breadth of the land, so that in city and tent the words rang out, "Blessed above women shall Jael, wife of Heber the Kenite be, blessed shall she be above women in the tent. . . ." But the tumult and the shouting died and Jael is now the woman who did something horrid with a tent nail.

These two women—one in her isolated tent amongst the flocks on the plain of Zaanaim, the other in the civilised region between Ramah and Bethel, lived in turbulent times. The Hebrews, under the leadership of Joshua, had forced their way into Canaan, a land already settled and occupied by many tribes who resented and resisted the intrusion. Strong in the belief that this was the land which their God had promised to their forefather, Abraham, and intended for their enjoyment, the invaders had fought their way fiercely and mercilessly and succeeded in establishing themselves in many places. But they were far from controlling the country. Here they might be supreme, there upon sufferance, in another place they were—to the disgust of the Biblical historians—settling down and being absorbed by the tribes they were supposed to supplant. It was a critical time of flux and change, of destiny's ebb and flow, and the most dangerous thing of all—that the Jews should lose their sense of being a "peculiar" people and become merged with the heathen tribes about them—was a matter which was disturbing the minds of all thoughtful men. In fact the Biblical historian says frankly that it was *because* the Israelites were losing their sense of high and special destiny that Jabin, King of Canaan, was allowed to afflict them for twenty years, demanding they pay tribute to him, and sending fierce little punitive expeditions against them under the leadership of his great general, Sisera.

To the modern mind it seems astonishing that the Jews preserved as great a sense of nationalism and devotion to a common purpose as they actually did. Apart from Jehovah, a God of very recent revelation, invisible, incorporeal, difficult for the common man to understand, they had no leader of unquestioned authority, no centre of government, no tradition. Moses had given them the ten commandments, and the book of Levitical law was a guide to behaviour, and what authority was wielded at all was exercised rather by spiritual than temporal right through the instrumentality of the Judges.

These Judges were chosen by Jehovah upon apparently arbitrary grounds; the qualifications seemed to be a consciousness of Jehovah and a belief in Israel's future. Apart from that the Judges had little in common with one another. Jephthah was one—a good soldier; Samson—a roistering adventurer; Eli—a good, weak, unmilitary man; Samuel—an inspired seer: and as though to prove that the Judgeship of Israel rested upon no material grounds, a woman is included in their number. She was the only female Judge in Israel's history and she was anything but an Amazon, yet one of the greatest victories over the Canaanites was scored during her rule.

We are told little about Deborah as a person. She was married and lived in a pleasant spot in a house overshadowed by palm trees. It seems as though she had been "a Judge in Israel" because of her gift of prophecy.

This gift of prophecy was one highly respected in ancient times and the weight of evidence to prove that some men and women did possess it is difficult to ignore or treat with scepticism. Elijah said that the dogs should devour Jezebel by the walls of Jezreel, and he said it in the moment when she was at the peak of her power, the most influential woman in Israel, a queen, firmly established on the throne; some thirty years later the dogs did eat her, by the walls of Jezreel. That is only one instance of numerous fulfilled prophecies, too numerous, in fact, to be attributed to lucky guesses or great insight or to anything else but the "seeing eye." No confusing theories about time sequences had then been propounded, and in Israel a prophecy which was fulfilled was taken as evidence that its maker was in direct communication with Jehovah. And it was this psychic gift of being able to look into the future, and accurately to predict coming events, which lifted Deborah out of the general run of women and gave her influence in a sphere wider than her own household.

She was a poet, too, with a gift as genuine and spontaneous as David's; but in the early part of her story this fact is not revealed. But it is not as a prophetess nor as a poet that Deborah takes her place in Jewish history, it is as the person who instigated and organised the campaign that ended the twenty years' tyranny which Jabin had exercised over the tribes.

It must be noted that she was not pushed, a female figurehead, into the forefront of a rebellion caused by a great uprush of national feeling. The Jews had borne with Jabin and suffered under Sisera for twenty years and had fallen into the habit of hopeless fortitude. Alone, within the confines of her mind, in what she believed to be communion with her God, Deborah conceived the notion of setting Israel free.

It never occurred to her to lead the rebellion. She had no military knowledge, no precedent to go upon; and her very admiration of Jael's action proves her to have been of a squeamish nature. So she sent for the most likely man she could think of, Barak, an able, if somewhat uninspired, soldier, and told him that if he could raise an army of ten thousand men she could promise him that he would have a victory over Sisera.

Barak returned her an answer which has often been misconstrued; it was one which shows him to have been a man of supreme moral courage. Without quibble and without shame he said he would raise the army and go to the battle, but only if Deborah accompanied him. He knew that he lacked something, inspiration, leadership, spiritual force without which his military skill and his comparatively small force would be useless; and he was perspicacious enough to see that this woman possessed the thing he lacked.

Deborah said that she would go with him; and then, passing from a statement of fact to a forecast of the future, she added that all the honour of victory should not be Barak's, since the

mote people, holding themselves aloof from the politics and allegiances of the people of the little stone villages and small fortified towns. The pressure of Jabin's tax gatherers had never fallen upon them, they were too poor, too mobile, not worth the trouble of pursuing, so the rebellion which Deborah had raised would concern them little, if at all.

Amongst these dwellers on the plain was a man called Heber. He belonged to the Kenite tribe, and the Kenites were, on the whole, friendly to the Jews; they had accepted them and even shown kindness and as late as the reign of Saul we find this kindness remembered and the Kenites exempt from the general massacre ordered for the Canaanites. But Heber, perhaps for some private reason of his own did not share his tribe's attitude to the Hebrews; he was in favour of Jabin, and earlier in the day, when Sisera was marching upon Esdraelon, Heber had pointed out to him exactly where the Israelite force was mustering. So as Sisera stumbled, faint and exhausted, sick with defeat, on foot along the path over which in the morning his chariot had rolled, he knew that he had only to find a low black tent set in a stretch of pasture, dotted over with Heber's flocks and herds, and he would be safe. When he saw them he knew a lightening of the spirit. He had been defeated, but only by a chance storm; and he had escaped the holocaust of Esdraelon: Heber would give him food and a change of clothing, and lend him an ass or a camel, and soon he would be safe back in Hazor, explaining everything to his king and laying plans for another campaign.

So he thought. But Heber was not in the tent when Sisera reached it. Jael was there, alone. And what that meant the exhausted man never guessed. How could he? For she went out to meet him and said, "Turn in, my lord, turn in to me; fear not." A kind and reassuring welcome. What could there be to fear from one lone woman in an isolated tent, a woman moreover who was the wife of a proved adherent? Very willingly, very gladly Sisera laid himself down and allowed Jael to cover him, and bring him milk, and food, which she served from her best dish, "a lordly dish," in honour of his rank.

Soon, fed and comforted and hopeful again, he felt sleep steal upon him, so he said to Jael, "Stand in the door of the tent, and it shall be that when any man doth come and inquire of thee and say, Is any man here? that thou shalt say, No."

He had never mentioned the battle, nor had she asked him a question. His very presence there in the nomad's tent explained everything. Sisera in triumph would have been in his chariot, surging forward, carrying terror and destruction through the land as he had so often done in years past. There was no need for him to describe the victory of the rebellious Israelites.

Why Israel's cause should have been dear to Jael's heart is never disclosed. Her nationality is not mentioned; she is always "the wife of Heber the Kenite." But there is enough indirect evidence in the story to warrant the speculation that she may have been a Jewess who had married a man outside her own race. Such marriages were frequent, and the Old Testament historians always mention them with acrimony; and there is in the very repetition of the words "wife of Heber the Kenite" just a flavour of something that might be reproach. Not "Jael the Kenite," a phrase which underlines the oddness and opportune chance of her striking a blow for Israel, but always "wife of," a term which, if one thinks about it, suggests a certain difference of interests, if only a difference in the date of demise. However, Josephus, whose details about the "discomfiting" of the Canaanites, are valuable to the story, calls her simply "Jael, a Kenite," and that she may have been, one of the Kenites who were favourable towards the Jews. Heber, her husband, we are told, "had severed himself from the Kenites" and although Jael was, in duty bound, compelled to share his physical departure from his tribe she may have remained faithful to the majority opinion.

In any case her heart was with Israel; and in the light of her action in the evening of this momentous day one can imagine how bitterly she must have suffered during its morning when she was compelled to stand by, maintaining a wifely silence, while her husband pointed out the Israelites' rallying point in Mount Tabor to the enemy of the people she favoured. Probably then she had willed, with all the force of her violent nature, that Barak should not suffer defeat, that some miracle might avert the apparently inevitable. Now, as day declined, she gave the exhausted general her assurance that no man should enter the tent and take him unawares, and she drew the covers over him and watched him fall asleep, knowing that the enemy of Israel had put himself into her hands; and as his eyelids fluttered and his breathing grew quiet she looked backwards over the twenty years when he had been the terror of Israel; and forward to the time when he would return at the head of a new army; and she took her decision.

So now he sleeps, trustful as a child, and as seemingly harmless; asleep in the tent of the man he has proved his friend. And then the woman, Jael, strikes and becomes, for all time the woman who did something nasty with a tent peg. (Trite as it may be to do so one *must* think of Hitler. If he had lain down, trustfully, to sleep in the house of an anti-Nazi woman, in the middle of the war, what would the world have expected of her?)

It is, one can only suppose, the fact that she struck a sleeping man that has cast discredit upon her. That and the fact that she offered him a false sympathy, a false hospitality. But awake, and warned, Sisera, even in exhaustion would have been more than a match for her; he probably carried some arms and would have been no weakling. She took the only way open to a woman. And when she looked at him she saw, not a tired man who had trusted her and put himself under her protection, but the old enemy of Israel, miraculously in her power, momentarily in her power. And she knew that if she failed to strike he would "live to fight another day." She knew his record and could guess at his future. She knew about those forces, barely tapped, waiting in Hazor for their general's return. A single contingent of Jabin's army had been wiped out, by chance, upon the Plain of Esdraelon, but with Sisera safe and sound such a reverse would be forgotten in a matter of days. And she knew that Heber, that sympathiser with the Canaanites would soon be back, and that in this moment, between Sisera's falling asleep and her husband's return it was possible for her, and for her alone, to turn a simple temporary defeat into a smashing disaster. For more hung in those days upon a single man's reputation and prowess than we, in our more complicated times, can understand. (Goliath fell and thirty thousand Philistines fell with him.)

And chivalry, we must remember, was a thing yet unthought of. Jehovah himself, most merciful of all known gods, sent His people into battle with categorical orders to destroy the enemy root and branch, old men, women, little children, oxen and asses and kine, and was angry, as in the case of Saul and Agag, when the order was imperfectly carried out. And Jael was a realist, a woman who had lived close to nature all her life, and knew that a tired tiger will rise refreshed and be a tiger again, that a sleeping adder is a matter, not for sentiment, but for swift action.

So she reached out and took the only weapons which were to hand (the secret of all success), and with the tent peg in one hand and the hammer in the other she stole towards Sisera.

And the skull of the great general is softer and less resistant than the soil of Zaanaim into which, many and many a time she has been obliged to peg the tent in the evening when Heber is busy with his flock. "He was fast asleep and weary. So he died." And his last thought had been comfortable and hopeful. It was a merciful end in its way.

So the thing is done and Sisera will never trouble Israel again. How was it less a blow for Jehovah than the thrust of spears, the lunge of swords over there at Esdraelon? Why should Jael rank below Deborah who with the word "Up" launched a thousand, ten thousand, arrows through the air?

Deborah, one feels, could no more have struck that blow than Jael could have made the poem which commemorated it. When Deborah sang, "Blessed above women shall Jael the wife of Heber the Kenite be" . . . she put her hand to the nail and her right hand to the workman's hammer, and with the hammer she smote Sisera, she smote through his head. Yes, she smote through his temples, she was gloating, as all human beings gloat, over an action which she knew to be utterly outside her own performance. There sounds the exaltation over violence in one who had never struck a violent blow; the wish-fulfilment of the unblooded.

The one woman was capable of planning and ordering an action in which thousands of men were slaughtered; in retrospect she could exult over the striking of one decisive blow; but in Jael's place she could never have regarded Sisera with the single eye of hatred; the other could strike the blow, but she was incapable of the imaginative extension which Deborah's poem shows. For, amid all the jubilation, the triumphant nationalism of Deborah's poem, there is something too often ignored, something that is absent from much of Biblical poetry—an introspective approach to the defeated. "The mother of Sisera looked out at a window and cried through the lattice, Why is his chariot so long in coming? Why tarry the wheels of his chariot? Her wise ladies answered her, yea, she returned answer to herself . . ." One wonders how often Deborah, Judge of Israel, prophetess, seer, had been obliged to return answer to herself. How she must have respected Jael who asked herself no questions, Jael, who had no thought for Sisera's mother, threatened with sorrow, Jael who simply reached for the tent peg and the hammer and struck.

The two women are directly opposite, absolutely complementary in nature, and it took the two of them to free Israel from the threat of the Canaanites. Two women. Whether one man could have struck down Sisera and then included the mention of Sisera's mother in his commemorative poem it would be difficult and futile to debate. Walter Raleigh, perhaps? But then he was unsuccessful in everything he attempted, "a house divided against itself."

There is a great deal more that one would like to learn about this story. What did Heber say, and do, when he found that his ally of the morning had been killed in the evening by his wife? And did Deborah and Jael ever meet and stare at one another with mutual wonder and admiration and a vast respect for the other's unattainable qualities? . . . This is the woman who dared defy Sisera with a mere ten thousand men and count upon victory and then write that poem; this is the woman who held the peg steady while the blood spurted and the bone broke. Who shall answer these questions?

But if they walk in the land of shades together, they will not, I think, resent this linking of their names.

DELILAH

AUTHORIZED VERSION: *Judges 14:1-16:31*

> *"Howso great man's strength be reckoned,*
> *There are two things he cannot flee.*
> *Love is the first, and Death the second."*
>
> (*Kipling*: SIR RICHARD'S SONG)

Against the massive bar that turns the stones that grind the corn in the prison of Gaza a dozen pale captives yesterday pushed with all their strength until the muscles of their backs cracked and their skins were wealed by the overseer's whip. To-day, as though it weighed no more than a spindle, one man turns it. The hands that have, unweaponed, ripped life out of a raging lion now press against the insentient wood; the feet that were fleet enough to outstrip foxes go round and round in the dusty groove worn by the tread of the hopeless; the man who set wide fields of wheat ablaze because he was robbed of one woman now grinds out the yield of more and wider fields because a woman has robbed him.

Think of the laughter, unrestrained as the wind, loud as thunder that this mouth, hard-set in bitterness, has known; remember the power, the lust, the bucolic good humour, the joy in life that this automaton once knew. It does not matter that the tangled hair hangs so low, there are no eyes for it to trouble. Blind Samson is grinding the Philistine corn in Gaza and all because of Delilah.

Scholars say that the story of Samson—and therefore that of Delilah—was omitted from the early editions of the Book of

Judges but that later editors were forced to include it because Samson, though not a very spiritually inspiring Judge, was a very popular hero. That has a ring of truth for the story contains all the elements of a popular folk-tale and Samson has all the qualities of a hero of romance–superb physical strength, matchless daring, a robust sense of humor and a weakness for women. And his story, besides being easily understood by everyone who heard it, conformed to a traditional, very acceptable pattern. This man had luck in all his ventures, not only defeating his enemies but mocking them, until he became entangled with a traitress; after that he suffered a misery easily conceivable by the most torpid imagination; and after that the story curves up again to its astonishing yet inevitable and superbly stirring end.

It is very easy to see why the story of Samson and Delilah was popular, told and retold under the dusty, evening-gilded palms of summer and by the smoky winter fires of wood and camel dung. The Hebrew fathers probably emphasised its moral, pointing out to their sons what happened when a man "went a-whoring after strange women"; and the boys would swallow the extempore sermons for the sake of the jokes and the riddles, the slaying of the lion, the foxes with their firebrand tails and the fall of the pillars of Gaza.

Yet it is not as a story for boys, nor for the unsophisticated, that the story of Samson and Delilah has survived. Of all Old Testament romances this has made most impact upon the world of art. When Samson laid his head upon Delilah's lap innumerable notes of music stirred on the air, poems began to shape themselves, colours mingled upon a hundred palettes and, about formless blocks of stone, the chisels began to play. The rude untutored taste of a primitive people demanded that this story should be preserved in its sacred writings and since then musicians and sculptors and poets down the ages have recognised the rightness of that demand.

Delilah, who was to become the symbol of all that was at once seductive and false, was a Philistine. She lived at Sorek. The Old Testament does not say that she was a prostitute. Josephus, who dealt so tenderly with Rahab, calling her an innkeeper, says frankly that Delilah was a harlot and many things in her story point to his being right. Samson met her when he was, admittedly, a customer for bought favours.

When he first strode into Sorek and fell under her spell he was not a very young inexperienced man. He was, in fact, that oddly unromantic thing, a widower. Some time before he had married —to his parents' grief—a woman of Delilah's own race, and that at a time when the Philistines were enjoying one of their recurrent spells of dominance in Canaan, a time when it was more than ever morally incumbent upon the Jews to have no dealings with the enemy. But he had married the Philistine woman and lived with her happily until she betrayed to her own people the answer to the riddle which he had set them in order to despoil them. He had wagered them thirty sheets and thirty changes of raiment that they would not guess the answer to his riddle and, when they did guess it, he rapped out a sentence which shows him no fool. "If ye had not plowed with my heifer, ye had not found out my riddle," he said. But, the wager lost, he wasted no time in rebuking his wife but went off to gather his stake: he collected thirty changes of raiment from the bodies of thirty Philistines whom he killed in the streets of one of their chief cities—Askelon: and then he went back to his wife as though her treachery were a thing of no moment.

But his wife's more practically minded father had imagined that Samson would never live with her again and had married her off to another man. Samson, who had not minded losing his wager but did mind losing his wife, took his revenge upon the whole Philistine community by catching foxes, setting fire to their tails and turning them loose in the Philistine corn fields. Some of the farmers who had lost their corn worked out, with more coolness and accuracy than is usual with angry men, who was really to blame, and came up and in turn set fire to Samson's wife and her father.

Samson did not take another wife. But his experience had not cured him of his taste for Philistine women. He was not a welcome visitor in the cities of the Philistines and very often he made his visits at the risk of his life, but he became a frequenter of the harlots' quarters of the enemy cities. And it was there that he met Delilah.

One must assume that she was beautiful, or at least much skilled in the arts that give an illusion of beauty. Surely any woman who could so lightly dispense with the attentions of a lover like Samson must have been beautiful and much sought after. And the whole of her story seems to bespeak the harlot. The Philistine lords, as soon as they knew that the Hebrew giant frequented her house, came to her with the proposal that she should sell him to them—would even the lords of the Philistines have moved so boldly with any ordinary woman who had just taken a new lover? And would any ordinary woman have treated with them, as Delilah did, naming her price, eleven thousand pieces of silver from each without even a pretence at hesitation? The one consideration which might be held to mitigate her treachery does not arise; she was no patriot, the end of the story proves that beyond all doubt. Neither Samson nor the Philistine lords meant anything to her other than a means of obtaining money.

To Samson she meant a great deal. If the word "love" is too sweeping and complicated a term for his primitive emotion, we can at least say that he was infatuated by her. To visit her meant that he must enter his enemies' territory; he had been betrayed by a woman of her race before: and a good many of her actions would have roused suspicion in any lover less enchanted. Yet he trusted her implicitly to the very end of their association.

It is wrong, I think, to assume, as some writers do assume, that he always suspected her, and was on his guard, and gave her those deceptive answers to her questions out of self-defence. Could any love-making have gone on happily under the shadow of such a suspicion? And would he ever, even out of boredom, have told her the truth if he had dreamed the purpose to which she would put the information?

Delilah was skilful. The very phrasing of her question, "Tell me I pray thee, wherein thy great strength lieth and wherewith thou mightest be bound to afflict thee," has in it a naïveté that suggests, not the uneasy sparring of suspicion, but the completest intimacy. One can imagine her laying her little hand in his great one—Samson, you could crush my hand with one pressure of your fingers. You are so strong, I am so weak, suppose I were cross with you and wished to hurt you, how could I do it? The good-humoured, joking answer—Bind me with seven undried withies and you could do what you liked with me. All part of the joke that she should have seven undried withies ready for him upon his next visit; part of the joke to stand meekly, pretending to helplessness while she bound them about his great body. Best joke of all when she stood back and cried, "The Philistines be upon thee, Samson," and the superb muscles flexed and expanded and the withies broke like cotton threads. Imagine his laughter, shaking the house, and her plaintive cry—Ah, but you fooled me! He never guessed that the Philistines lay listening and waiting in an inner chamber, cautiously testing the result of the experiment, full of chagrin to hear laughter instead of bellows of distress. Nor did he suspect anything when Delilah repeated her question—But suppose I really wanted to hurt you, how could I do it? For one thing he must have been very used to the question; a thousand times he must have been asked the secret of his strength. For another he would never dream that she would wish to hurt him, this lovely, languorous, amorous creature who lay in his arms and accepted his love-making and shared his jokes and his laughter. It would amuse him, the strong man who never suffered hurt at anyone's hands to pretend to lie helpless under hers. So he told her to try seven new ropes, and when they failed to hold him, to try weaving some of his long hair into the web of her loom. It became part of the buffoonery which came so naturally to him; a light playful interlude in serious love-making.

But at last he was bored. For Delilah, with all that silver at stake, the game was serious; for him it was only a game, and there came an evening when he was weary, or in a mood for love undiluted by sport and the old silly question palled upon him. So he took her in his arms and lay on her bed and told her the truth—that since his birth he had been a Nazarite and that his hair had never been cut. He believed that to be the secret of his strength and that if he were shaven he would become weak and like other men.

The whole atmosphere of the tale changes then. It is significant that Delilah did not immediately leap up and make play with the scissors as she had done with the withies, the ropes and the loom. She was experienced about men, and something in his manner told her that now at last she had the truth. The secret was no more mentioned between them, but when he had gone she sent for the Philistine lords and demanded her money. She had never done that before. Philistines had lain concealed in her inner room on the chance that the trick might work, but this time, before ever the trick was tried, the lords came up with the money in their hands. They, too, trusted Delilah. And they, too, were in their turn betrayed.

She kept to the letter of her bargain. Next time Samson came striding down from the hills of Judah to visit her, she enticed him to put his head in her lap, and she soothed him to sleep by the touch of her long fingers in his hair. He slept as heartily as he did everything else and, while he slept, Delilah signalled for the man with the shears to enter, and one by one the crisp coarse locks of hair, the symbols of dedication and of favour, were severed, and when the giant waked to Delilah's teasing, he waked as other men, vulnerable as he had never been before. Even the old cry, "The Philistines be upon thee, Samson," could rouse him only to ordinary resistance, easily overwhelmed. So the lords of the Philistines entered and took him away; and one of the last sights that his eyes ever saw was the hard mocking face of the woman he had loved. Her feet were tangled in the fallen hair, her hands heavy with silver.

She did not bother, as they led him away, to tell them his secret. A few words, however laconically uttered, would have kept Samson helpless in their hands for the rest of his life, and left the pillars of Gaza to the hand of time to destroy. But Delilah did not say, "Keep his head shaven." The secret was hers, and she was a harlot; she never gave anything away. She had given those who had bargained with her exactly what they had bargained for, Samson delivered powerless into their hands; and that they had—not a pennyweight more.

They put out his eyes and set him to turn the mill stones in the gaol at Gaza. And out of his misery, out of the strength made impotent, the spirit of freedom chained, came one, at least, immortal line. . . . "Eyeless, in Gaza, at the mill with slaves."

Many imaginative versions of Delilah's behaviour have been offered us. In one she visits the prison, and the blind man who had loved her hears her steps and smells her perfume and is tormented into the actions of madness which his gaolers found so entertaining; in another she misses him, finds, too late, that she loved him, and suffers agonies of remorse. Somehow this woman, even her very name, is provocative of fancy. But, in the absence of authoritative guidance it is safe and reasonable to say that for some time she never thought of him again, except as the man whose betrayal had made her rich. It is even possible—for she was a woman, after all—that there was, somewhere, some man whom she did love, and who profited by those pieces of silver. One feels that if she had suffered any remorse, the story, which is an artistic masterpiece, would have mentioned it. She drove a harder bargain than Judas, but for her there was no Potters Field. For her there was a better house in Sorek, or more furniture for the house she had, and clothes and jewels and perfumes and the thing which perhaps she had always longed for, independence in a precarious world.

But the day was coming when she was to be reminded of Samson. His name was to be, once again as in the old days, upon every Philistine tongue. For having blinded and shackled him, the Philistines thought that he was in their power forever, and at the next festival of Dagon their god, when they had offered special sacrifices in gratitude for their deliverance from this Israelitish scourge they were inspired to send to the prison for Samson and make sport of him.

Hundreds of men and women, to whom in the past his name had brought a pang of terror, now crowded to see him, to gloat over his impotence, to wonder at his size and to speculate, with delicious horror, over what might happen if his former power were for one moment restored to him.

The pleasure to be derived from the enjoyment of danger-in-safety is a very fundamental thing; it sends people to the barred cages of menageries, to the tiered circus seats. Very close to it lies the pleasure to be gained from the sight of crippled strength made mad by rage; for that bulls and bears have been baited, chained lunatics teased. In the sport which the Philistines made of Samson, once their dreaded enemy, now their prisoner, both base pleasures were combined, and they taunted and teased him until they were weary. He was a suitable subject too. There was a good deal of the animal in him; until the very end he lacked dignity; his very impotence would madden him, without any taunting from the Philistines; for he would remember slaying the lion with his hands, and the mighty slaughter he had once wrought with no better weapon than an ass's jawbone.

The sport in the great house of Dagon ended. The boy—such a proud little Philistine—whose flattering duty it was to lead this blind and shackled terror from place to place, now led his charge aside to rest in a space between the pillars which were the king-posts of the house. Samson probably wept as he stood there, humbled, reduced. And the Philistine boy, who would be fond of his charge in the strange, unimaginative way in which circus attendants become fond of their erstwhile-dangerous beasts, would stare and wonder, remembering the lion and the thirty Philistines of Askelon and the riddles and the story of the betrayal and all the whole colourful dramatic story which seemed to end here in futile madness.

Presently Samson asked the boy to guide his hands so that he might feel the pillars of the house and lean against them. The boy did so, obligingly, never dreaming that he was at that moment posing the model for a picture which artists in paint and stone and word were to attempt again and again all down the centuries. And neither the boy nor any other Philistine in the whole of that great multitude noticed that as Samson's hands were guided to the pillars the blind man lifted his head and that the shaggy hair had stirred against his thick neck and brushed the bare, muscle-corded shoulders.

For Samson's hair had grown again: and in the whole of the land of the Philistines only one careless woman down in a house in Sorek could have known that that growth had any significance.

In the crowded house some other sport went forward, and Samson, in the quiet space between the pillars prayed his most human prayer; a prayer of which three words must strike a note of personal reminiscence in the mind of everyone who has ever prayed—as who has not, at some time or another? "Oh, Lord God, remember me, I pray thee, and strengthen me, I pray thee, only this once." *Only this once*. Let probability, possibility, reason, the law of nature, the law of man be just this once superceded in my favour; the base of almost every human prayer.

Having prayed that he added, "Let me die with the Philistines." For he knew that there would be no more hunting, no more fighting, no more jokes, no more love of women. Between the moment when he lifted his head from Delilah's lap to the moment when he set his hands on the pillars of the house in Gaza he had learned despair, and death is the only logical conclusion of despair. So gladly, for the last time, he braced his great muscles and knew, for one wild, exultant moment that strength had come back to him. Did he think, as he tested his hold upon the great stone columns, of the woman who had wormed out his secret and then kept it to herself? Thanks to her treachery, a moment since he had been a subject for sport; thanks to her reticence, his enemies were now at his mercy again.

The pillars bowed like reeds, and the night was filled with the sound of horrified screaming, the dust and the thud of falling masonry.

One feels, in this twentieth century, from a dispassionate distance, that, despite the commentators' doubts, there must have been truth in that story. Anyone inventing it could not have refrained from numbering Delilah amongst "the dead which he slew at his death." So perfect an example of the revenge, which Wilde called "rough justice," could not have been resisted by a mere spinner of stories. But there is never a hint of it. And we are left free to think that Delilah in her Sorek house, secure with the wealth and independence, would hear the news of the disaster and pause for a moment and remember Samson, not as the great blithe man who had come down from the Hebrew village with laughter and strange boasting tales and jests to make love to her,

every normal girl has at some time or another fitted herself. It is too common for notice. And so, despite the jokes about the relationship, is devotion between mother-in-law and daughter-in-law. So there is nothing noteworthy in the story of Ruth and Naomi save those words wrung out of a simple peasant girl under the stress of great emotion. As she spoke them Ruth became, for all time, a poet, standing for a moment in her own right, free of Naomi's dominance. Then the shadow engulfed her again and she went on into Bethlehem-Judah as a mere woman, a faithful daughter-in-law. And it would have surprised Naomi if anyone had told her, on that beautiful morning of harvest-time, that it was not for herself, nor for her husband, nor for her two sons that she would be remembered, but that she too would be immortal because of a single sentence spoken by Ruth.

The image of the worshipped always gives us a clue to the nature of the worshipper, so Naomi herself merits a little attention. She was a Jewess of Bethlehem-Judah, and she was married to a man named Elimelech, who, when there was a famine in Israel, emigrated to the land of Moab, taking with him his wife and his two sons. She makes it extremely plain—by words from her own mouth—that she was one of those numerous women who distinguish very sharply between men and women; not so much that they prefer the one to the other as that they hardly regard male and female as belonging to the same species.

When she moved into the land of Moab she "went out full"; she had three men belonging to her. When she went back to her native land she came "home again empty," because her men had gone and she had only a woman by her side. And although that woman had just uttered the most whole-hearted vow of devotion which ever lay upon human lips, Naomi did not hesitate, in her presence, without apology to describe herself as "empty and bitter." Another kind of woman might have said, laying her arm upon Ruth's shoulder, "I have one comfort left, God has been good in that He has given me a faithful daughter-in-law." But no such thought would have occurred to Naomi. She was a man's woman and she reckoned her wealth in men.

Therefore, when she arrived in Moab with Elimelech and

Mahlon and Chilion, she was, despite the emigration which had been forced upon her, a happy, contented woman. And when Mahlon and Chilion chose to marry Moabitish women, she welcomed in their wives with the serene confidence and gentle dignity of the completely established and emotionally satisfied. It was so that Ruth saw her first and began to love her. The young girl who adores an elder woman almost always does so because the woman excels at something towards which she herself has some ambition; and there was Naomi, the perfect wife and mother, a very attractive model for the Moabitish girl who had married outside her own tribe and was, perhaps, a trifle unsure of her ground. Naomi, then, had all the charm of the well-protected, the graciousness of the fortunate, the tolerance of the experienced, and Ruth came to love her more than she realised.

Elimelech died, and Naomi's supremacy might then have been threatened had either of her daughters-in-law borne a child. But neither did; and after a time both Mahlon and Chilion died too and the three women were left alone. Naomi then showed the virtue of consistency. She made no attempt to build up a new life around her daughters-in-law They were young women who, with any luck, might marry again; she herself was "too old to have a husband," so she faced resolutely the fate of a widow in eastern society. She intended to go back to her own land and her kinsmen and find there, in some house, the humble place, the corner and the crust which was all a woman without a man could hope for.

She announced her intention to Ruth and Orpah, and both young women offered to accompany her part of the way. It seems inconceivable that Naomi could have lived with Ruth over a period of time and not been aware of her devotion, or have failed to see the difference between her and Orpah; yet at this moment she treated them exactly alike. Did she not know that behind the veil and the robe of Orpah beat a merely kind heart, and that behind the veil and the robe of Ruth a heart was breaking, racked with love, torn by apprehension, sinking in despair and bounding with desperate decision. Ruth was suffering the same impulse to self-immolation as has sent men into exile in the train of dethroned royalty. She had known Naomi, and loved her in the days of her good fortune, she could not now abandon her. She must have known Naomi well enough to have realised that, being a woman, she could be of no real value to her, but she knew that she could, by faithful service, ease the path of loneliness.

So when Naomi halted at last and said they must both go back to their own land and their families, Ruth made her decision.

They had reached the point where, far away, far below, the fields of Judah showed, flooded golden with the barley harvest—(those same fields whose thin and blighted crops had driven Naomi and her family into exile ten years before; ah, ten years ago how different was her state; oh, Elimelech, oh, Mahlon and Chilion, my husband and my sons!)

The moment of parting had come, and Naomi drew both young women to her, and kissed them, and praised them both equally, saying that they had dealt kindly with the dead and with her. And she wished them, equally, the best thing which it was within the power of her mind to conceive, that they would both find husbands and rest in their husbands' houses.

It was a moment heavy with memories of the happy days they had shared, days of little shared duties and little shared jokes, with Elimelech and Mahlon and Chilion coming in from the fields in the evening to the meal which the women had prepared and all the peace of a well-run household. Day after day, through all the seasons' changes, a time never to be known again. Naomi knew that her life, as a woman, was ended, and even Orpah may have wondered whether the future would ever bring her anything so sweet; as for Ruth, she was distraught. When Orpah kissed Naomi and then stood back, her face already turned towards her own people and her own gods, Ruth "clave to her." Orpah knew the best chance of another husband lay where one was known, where one's family would help with the matchmaking. But Ruth, who had known Naomi in the days of her glory, thought, she has no husband, she has no son, she has nobody but me!

Psychologists might argue that it showed a masculine trait in

Ruth to be so devoted to, and to feel so responsible for, another woman. And one might agree that the best women do have a masculine trait, as the best men have a feminine one. Yet Ruth had been a perfectly satisfactory wife, or Naomi would have let her know about it; and her subsequent behaviour, over the matter of Boaz, was feminine enough.

At that moment she was sexless; for her poem is sexless. Clinging to Naomi she said, "Intreat me not to leave thee, nor to return after following thee: for whither thou goest I will go; and where thou lodgest I will lodge: thy people shall be my people, and thy God, my God: where thou diest I will die, and there will I be buried: the Lord do so to me and more also, if aught but death part thee and me."

"*Das Volk dichtet.*" For it is a poem; and its maker could, very probably, neither read nor write. They were words of pure emotion, spontaneous, unconsidered; and they express most perfectly a sentiment of devotion that has never been bettered. Lyrical, rhythmical, they beat upon the air with a note of eternity, one thing, perfectly expressed, for all time.

Naomi said nothing. "When she saw that she was steadfastly minded to go with her she left speaking unto her." Not one word of reciprocal devotion, no promise of reciprocal affection. Is it too much to imagine that as they began to walk down towards the fields of Judah, Naomi was thinking that now there were two of them, two useless, female creatures, to seek hospitality of her kin, that the awkward situation was made even more awkward, and that it would have been far better for Ruth to turn back and seek her family's aid in her search for a second husband?

Whatever she may have thought she said nothing; and so they went on together and came at last to Naomi's native city. And there her friends and her kinsmen came out to welcome her back, and called her by her name, and she said, "Call me not Naomi, call me Mara, for the Almighty hath dealt very bitterly with me." A heart's brimming chalice had been offered to her, there was a shoulder to lean upon, hands braced to work for her, a mind open for her slightest direction; but heart, mind, shoulder and hands were those of a woman; to Naomi they had no value at all.

It was not until the two women had settled again in Bethlehem, and Naomi had taken stock of her kinsmen, that Ruth assumed some importance in her eyes. Not for herself, not for her devotion, but because she was a personable young female, capable of attracting some man. And by that time the two women had experienced enough of hardship to prove that Naomi's view of masculine importance was a view rooted upon a valid argument, not a perverse nature. In that profoundly simple and unspecialised system of society there were so pitiably few things that a woman could do to earn her own living. Every household, with its plurality of wives, its daughters, daughters-in-law, orphaned female relatives, concubines and—where there was wealth to spare—a bondmaid or two, was completely self-sufficient. All the necessary woman's work could be performed by the women of the family and there were plenty of hands for every job. Nobody would pay Ruth and Naomi to cook or clean, to spin or weave, to sew, or to tend children. And outside the household there was nothing a woman could do save become a prostitute. There were no shops or offices in those days. If they failed to establish themselves under some man's protection, in however humble a capacity, Ruth and Naomi were bound to fall into utter destitution, for even the seasonal field work, which only the young and strong could perform, would not offer reward enough or sufficiently steady employment to keep two women for any length of time.

However, Naomi's return to Bethlehem coincided with the barley harvest, and that was one of the times when women were welcome in the fields, so Ruth, to provide bread for herself and her mother-in-law went out to glean.

The Old Testament says that "it was her hap to light" on a field belonging to Boaz; but the statement comes so hard upon the heels of a description of this man, his mighty wealth and his kinship to the dead Elimelech that one cannot avoid a wonder whether a little feminine guile did not influence that chance. For Levitical law was not blind to the disadvantages of women in a primitive society and expressly ordered that "kinsmen"—a word given a wide range—should take widows under their protection; and it may have been that this rich kinsman had been the lodestar to draw Naomi back to Bethlehem. And she may have thought that two women were a heavy burden to thrust upon any man, and so refrained from approaching him directly.

However, Ruth chanced to light upon the field belonging to Boaz, and he noticed her and took her under his protection. For she was, after all, an alien, not merely to Bethlehem but to Israel, and might have met with a sorry welcome from some nationalistic young harvesters. But Boaz told her that he had heard how good she had been to her mother-in-law; and he invited her to share the meal which he had provided for his work-people, and he even went to the length of telling his young men who were reaping to cast down a handful of corn every now and again in her path, so that her gleaning might be a rich one. So Ruth returned that evening, not only with a good supply of corn, but with a story that would sound very pleasant in Naomi's ears. A glimmering hope lightened her bitter emptiness. Boaz was a kinsman, he was wealthy, he had already shown himself interested in the Moabitess; upon such a foundation what might not a clever woman build?

She may have evolved, and rejected, several plans during the next few days when Ruth was gleaning with the maidens of Boaz. But in her final plan there shows the age-old wisdom, combined with a certain ruthlessness which is essentially feminine, and the natural heritage of women like Naomi. She knew that there were two essential things; Boaz must, for once, see Ruth at her best, not attired for field work, but properly robed and anointed; and there must be provoked between them, by force if necessary, a situation more intimate and compromising than the easy give and take of the open corn fields.

So she waited until the harvest was gathered and the night of the threshing came. Then she told Ruth to put on her finest raiment and go down to the barn when Boaz was threshing; not to reveal herself until the man had eaten and drunken—and threshing barley with a flail would be thirsty work—and when he lay down to rest to go and lie at his feet. "And he will tell thee what thou shalt do." Naomi had no doubt that Boaz, already attracted, thrust into physical proximity, a little drunk perhaps, would have some suggestion to make to the Moabitess.

Ruth trusted her mother-in-law implicitly. Perhaps she was already a little bewildered by the strange customs of this strange place and therefore looked upon Naomi as a guide through the maze; or she may have thought that Naomi's judgement upon every subject would be better than her own. She said meekly, "All that thou sayest unto me I will do." And she carried out Naomi's instructions to the letter.

So she went to the barn, and went through the ritual of claiming kinship, which, even if strictly allowable by Levitical law, was a custom so rarely followed as to be a little unconventional. Boaz himself, though delighted with the girl, and flattered beyond measure to think that she had chosen him rather than some younger man, and though he intended next day to follow the ritual to its correct conclusion, was evidently aware that he had been compromised. For he sent Ruth away before it was light enough for faces to be recognised, and said, "Let it not be known that a woman came into the floor."

He did not send her away empty; he poured into her veil as much corn as it would hold, six measures of barley; and Ruth, as she made her way back through the grey dawn to the place where Naomi waited, knew that, whatever other outcome the evening's bold venture might have, at least it had staved off actual hunger for a while.

Naomi had higher hopes. She listened to Ruth's account and then said, with the confidence of a woman who has made men her life study, "Sit still, my daughter, until thou know how the matter will fall; for the man will not rest until he have finished the thing this day."

And she was, as usual, right. The thing which had withheld Boaz from taking full advantage of the Levitical right of a kinsman with a widow, was the fact that he knew of the existence of a closer relative, who must, by the same Levitical law, have the first offer of the Moabitess as a wife. With the first light of day he set to work to find this man and ask him whether he intended to exercise his right. But he put it craftily. He gathered a senate of elders at the city gate, and in their presence asked this nearer kinsman of Naomi's whether he was prepared to redeem a piece of land upon which the dead Elimelech and his dead sons had some claim. And he pointed out that such redemption—such an open performance of a kinsman's duty—carried with it the right to marry Ruth, the widow of one of the claimants. The kinsman who probably had women enough and land enough of his own to handle, said that he could not redeem the land because to do so would mar his own inheritance and openly, in public, before all the elders, he handed over to Boaz all his rights in the matter.

Nowhere else in the story is there any mention of the land that must be redeemed, and one is free to fancy that it existed only in Boaz's imagination. But the law was satisfied, and so were the elders when he said gravely that he would assume responsibility both for the redemption of the land and the welfare of Ruth.

Whether Ruth loved Boaz, whether she had loved the dead man, Mahlon, no one now can say. In that country and in that time the emotional vagaries of women were given little heed. But we do know that she loved Naomi, and however she viewed her marriage to Boaz, we can be certain that even her passive acceptance of an arranged plan—after all, the common lot of the Eastern woman—would be lightened and sweetened into glad acquiescence by the thought that now she could provide Naomi with a more worthy home, reinstate her as a woman with a man in her family, and make sure her future.

Actually she was to do more than that. For in due time Naomi —through Ruth—achieved the final crown of Eastern womanhood. Ruth bore Boaz a son, and so Naomi became, by virtue of a family tie far closer knit than ours, a grandmother. The child was only the son of her daughter-in-law by her second marriage, according to our lights; but those women, of an older, perhaps wiser time, took it and laid it in Naomi's bosom and said, "There is a son born to Naomi." In that situation shines the silver lining of the cloud of female oppression, of the forced marriage, the utter dependence upon men; in some ways, vital ways, these women were rich. By our standards Naomi would have had no claim at all to Ruth's son; by their standards she possessed him.

There were no kings, there was no thought of kings in Israel at that time, and by the cradle of Ruth's son there was no one with a mind so farreaching, so far-leaping as to dream that he would be the grandfather of a king. Nobody there could imagine that the child whom they named Obed would be the father of Jesse, the father of David. Obed's birth was celebrated worthily; for they would see, these Hebrew men and women, called to the feast, that Boaz's adherence to the law, Ruth's fidelity to her mother-in-law, had been rewarded, they could look forward far enough to see Obed inheriting his father's wealth and in turn begetting his sons and sharing in his grandsons. But of the holy oil of anointing, of the harp music in a haunted palace, of Goliath slain by a stone from a sling, of the crown of Israel and the conquest of Jerusalem no one in Bethlehem could prophesy that day.

Yet one Goliath was slain there, by that cradle, though it was to be centuries before his death was admitted. Some simple, pleased, possibly sycophantic woman placed the baby in Naomi's arms, and said, not knowing the weight of her own words, or the deafness of the ears upon which they fell, a sentence which is an epitaph of the inferiority of women, "Thy daughter-in-law, which loveth thee, which is better to thee than seven sons, hath borne him."

Better than seven sons! One sees Naomi staring across that precious male baby head at Ruth, and with what astonishment, what profound disbelief.

Chapter 11

MICHAL

AUTHORIZED VERSION: I *Samuel 16:12*—II *Samuel 6:23*

"Love me no more, now let the god depart
If love be grown so bitter to your tongue!"
(*Edna St. Vincent Millay*: FATAL INTERVIEW)

The story of Michal and David opens in the land of faery and ends in the dry dust of psychology. It is a familiar pattern. There are many books in which, as the story advances, a certain light seems to fail and die and, at the end, one is left thinking how sad it is that a thing which started so well should have ended so badly; and one cannot bear to look back again at the bright beginning, and is sad for an hour. To such stories this one belongs.

It opens in the palace of the king of Israel where a neurotic man finds solace in the harp music of a shepherd boy, and a young princess hovers in the background, feasting her eyes and her ears and falling in love. It ends with a hard-mouthed woman saying bitter words to another king made dizzy by a music not his own.

Michal was the daughter of Saul, the first king of Israel. The twelve tribes, slowly soldering themselves into a nation, had abandoned the rule of the Judges. Samuel, the last of the line, unwillingly and with dire warnings, had anointed Saul, who was not only Jehovah's choice but also the natural choice of a primitive people, in that he was physically the pick of all the tribesmen, a likely warrior and a man of certain spiritual perceptiveness.

Saul, in his early days of kingship, seemed likely to fulfil his promise, for he planned and conducted successful campaigns against several indigenous Canaanite tribes who resisted the establishment of the Jews as a nation. But in the flush of success he disobeyed Jehovah's direct command and, over the matter of the Amalekites' property, proved himself to be greedy and materialistic. The divine favour was withdrawn from him and he became conscious of his loss and was troubled by what the Bible calls "an evil spirit from the Lord"—a vastly significant statement. And if one chooses to understand that, as middle age encroached, Saul lost his vigour and his ambition and his courage and drifted into a form of melancholia not far removed from madness, that is only putting the same situation into another mould of words.

A new champion of Jewish nationalism was needed—and found. Saul's son was passed over, and before he died old Samuel was sent to perform another anointing, this one a secret. The sacred oil was smeared upon the smooth boyish brow of David, the youngest son of a substantial sheep farmer of Bethlehem. Saul was still king, but his house was doomed and his successor already chosen.

Some premonition of disaster may have visited him, for his melancholy, his evil spirit, increased and his desperate servants, searching for some palliative, suggested harp music as a means of exorcism. Who could provide it? Was there not a shepherd boy of Bethlehem with a reputation as a maker of sweet music and as a singer of songs? So they mentioned his name to Saul, and Saul sent to Jesse, David's father, and the proud farmer sent his son with his harp and a present of bread and meat and wine, down to Gibeah where the king had his palace. And perhaps to Jesse and to David who knew about that secret anointing, this movement from sheep farm to palace seemed just a step on the predestined road: but to Saul David's arrival would be without ulterior significance. The new harpist had come; let there be music.

The first meetings between the king and the king-to-be were pleasant ones, marred by no shadow of jealousy. Even Jesse's offering of food and wine was acceptable to the king of a poor, pastoral people; and David's music delighted him. Probably Saul, tormented, hag-ridden man, saw in the handsome young shepherd the ghost of his own youth; for he too had been a handsome young man, full of vigour and confidence: and their upbringings had been almost identical. When Samuel had met Saul and anointed him he had been searching for his father's asses; David had tended his father's sheep. So simple and direct was the step from the farm to the throne in those days. And the harp music proved to be effective. Saul was cheered and comforted and so pleased with his new musician that he sent a message to Jesse saying that he found David indispensable and intended to give him a proper appointment as his armour-bearer.

It is likely that during this happy period Michal saw David for the first time. Elaborate palace procedure and court etiquette had not yet been evolved by the Jews and there would be nothing to prevent the young princesses, Merab and Michal, from listening to the wonderful music made by the young man from Bethlehem. And the beautiful young man who could accompany his music with songs of his own making, who had easy good manners and an air of confidence and high destiny, proved as attractive to Saul's daughters and son as to the king himself. It is part of the tragedy of this story that three of the members of this doomed family should love the man who was to supplant them. Saul's later hatred and ferocity had its roots in a love that had rotted; Jonathan's affection for him has become a by-word; Michal married him and risked her life to save him. And as the shepherd boy's brown fingers plucked at the strings, and his voice lifted in song, he must, sometimes, have remembered the old prophet and the oil and the anointing and known that one day he would sit in Saul's place. So towards the listening princesses his eyes would turn with an unabashed appreciation, which they, in their innocence of the secret, would find all the more entrancing in a shepherd boy.

But this first happy visit to court was not prolonged, and so far as David and Michal were concerned nothing more than an exchange of glances, bold and languishing, had happened. The Philistines, against whom the Israelites had waged intermittent warfare for many years, gathered a fresh army, and with a new champion ready to challenge any Israelite who dared venture into the field against him, opened a new campaign. Three of Jesse's older sons joined the army and the democratic rule of the day empowered him to call David, the king's armour-bearer, back to the farm to help with the sheep. And if, during this quiet rural interval, the shepherd boy dreamed of marrying a king's daughter, his dreams would have centred about Merab. For Merab was the king's elder daughter, that traditional, fairy prize held out to enterprising young men since the beginning of all legends. It may be that it was with an eye upon Merab that David accepted the challenge of the Philistine champion, Goliath of Gath.

He was with the army on that particular morning upon a peaceful and humble errand. Jesse had sent down some supplies for his soldier sons and had entrusted David to deliver them into the fighting line. Every child knows the story of the next hour of that day, and how the overgrown creature who had kept all the Hebrews paralysed with terror appeared to the shepherd boy to be merely an excellent target for his sling, the weapon with which he had practiced during the long monotonous hours of sheep-tending back in Bethlehem.

But that slung stone slew more than the Philistine champion; it killed the happy relationship between Saul and his young musician. For as soon as they saw Goliath defeated the Philistines fled in panic, and the Jews, strong in their confidence in Jehovah now that He had sent them a deliverer, pursued their enemies and indulged in one of those ruthless, wholesale slaughters which, though logical and perhaps necessary to their own survival, make unhappy reading. Thirty thousand Philistines, we are told, died that day and the pursuit drove on as far as the two chief cities, Gath and Ekron, which were thoroughly sacked.

The credit for that triumphant day went to David, and Michal was far from being alone in her adoration of him. Half the women in Israel were in love with him then; and it was their enthusiasm which enlightened Saul. They came out to meet the young hero, chanting "Saul has slain his thousands and David his tens of thousands" and for Saul everything was changed. He might be, as he showed himself to be, genuinely grateful to the young man who had slain the terror and ended, with one stroke, a long war of nerves; he might reward him and praise him; but he could never like him again. For how could he listen to those singing women and not remember the time, not so long past, when he had been a hero too, when his conquests had been lauded in the streets and the power of confident leadership had reposed in him? And could he avoid the thought that it should have been himself, the crowned, chosen leader of Israel, to offer at least to confront Goliath?

There was at first no open enmity. The war was over, Jesse's older sons returned to Bethlehem and David stayed on at Gibeah, still trying to please and soothe Saul with his music. But Saul "eyed David from that day and forward" and now that he hated the maker of the music the harp lost its curative quality. Even as David plucked melody from its strings Saul's evil spirit triumphed and on two separate occasions moved him to throw his javelin across the music-filled room, intending to pin David against the wall. Twice David escaped, and probably there escaped with him a rumour of the king's malady, a rumour that would widen and darken as time went on.

When the mad moment had passed Saul promoted David and made him captain over a thousand men. This action was dictated by a neurotic mixture of motives. Partly he would wish to compensate for his lapse into frenzy; partly he would wish for an excuse to get the young hero out of his palace, his city and his sight; partly he hoped that a young, inexperienced soldier, suddenly raised to authority would make a fool of himself in the eyes of all Israel. But David "behaved himself very wisely," and his popularity grew.

So Saul cast about for a means of making this cautious young man reckless, and his eyes rested upon his two daughters. Merab was the elder, the more glittering prize; so when David, summoned into the dangerous presence again, came, Saul promised him that if he were valiant and active in warfare he would give him Merab for his wife. So one of the dreams dreamed on the sunny pastures of Bethlehem had almost come true. But the promise was never kept.

No conclusive reason for Saul's change of mind is given us,

and it is possible to accept sheer spite as a reason for Saul's breaking of the promise, and marrying Merab to Adriel the Mehothalite. But is it safe to overlook the possibility that Michal had a hand in the business? She was in love with David. She was, as the later events in the story prove, a crafty and resourceful young woman. She could play, successfully, a very double game. Even after her marriage to David she retained to a surprising extent her father's confidence. Is it too much to suspect that during this period, while she endured the torture of knowing that David was risking his life many times over in order to qualify for marriage with Merab, Michal applied some of her cunning to the business of getting David for herself? Was it she who suggested to Saul, who was neurotically suggestible, that marriage to Merab would strengthen his rival, marriage to herself weaken him? They must at least have talked the matter over and she must have acted and spoken with deceptive falsity, for when Saul was told that his second daughter loved David he was delighted and said, "I will give him her that she may be a snare to him." What sort of snare, and for whom, the king was to discover to his cost.

So Michal married David.

He was to have so many wives, this second king of Israel; and to so many of them a story was to adhere for all time. There was Abigail, whose shortsighted, drunken husband, Nabal, refused sustenance to the exiled David in a moment of extremity. She was to ride out with the offering her husband withheld and was to be Nabal's widow and David's wife within a space of a few days. There was Bathsheba who was to take her innocent bath, be the death of her husband, Uriah, and go up to the palace to bear Solomon. Women were important in David's life; in his last days, with the chill of death upon him, they were to bring the beautiful young Shunamite, Abishag, to his couch in the hope that the old fire would kindle. But Michal was his first wife: and in marrying her he received honour. Afterwards he bestowed it. He was Michal's lover in a very special sense, for she had his untried youth. And he respected her. At a critical moment he obeyed her implicitly; there is no other record of his putting himself into human hands, a passive taker of orders. She may have stood to him as a symbol of an ambition attained, as a pledge of the validity of that secret anointing. She was certainly his superior in sophistication, a thing which matters to a young man. Saul may have kept his father's asses as David his father's sheep but Michal was a princess, reared in a palace, skilled in intrigue. Did they laugh together, in the evenings when, his military duties done, he came back to their house, over Saul's credulity, Saul's madness, Saul's animosity? Did he tell her about Samuel's visit to the sheep farm, and did she realise that she would in time be queen of Israel while Merab was merely the wife of Adriel? They were, after all, a young couple, married, with all the shared secrets and jokes and intimacies that marriage implies.

But their happy days together were very few. Jonathan, Michal's brother, had managed to patch up a precarious truce between Saul and David and once again David played his harp in the king's presence. And once again Saul's hand strayed to his javelin and once again David escaped from the presence of his would-be murderer. But this time the simple removal of his presence was not enough and when he reached his own house—with a fine tale to tell his wife about her father's behaviour—Michal told him that the house was already being watched, that he had entered it as a rat enters a trap and that, unless he managed to escape in the night, by the morning he would be killed.

It was not, for her, an easy situation. She was still in her father's confidence, and though that may have seemed amusing and interesting while the truce between Saul and David held, the moment had come when she must face reality and choose between her father and her husband. And as she betrayed Saul she may have remembered the days of her youth when Saul had been cheerful and confident and kind, a hero to his children as to the whole nation. But she loved David. So now that the double game had ended and she was obliged to decide upon a course of action, she put her long-practiced craft and subtlety at his service.

She could not flee with him; for she must stay behind to gain time; and there would be no place for her in the life which he must hitherto lead as a hunted outlaw in the hills and the caves and the waste places. So she let him down through a window; her heart fluttering with nervousness and apprehension, her eyes full of tears, her delicate palms seared by the rope. And David may have wept too, he was a man of easy emotions. As his feet touched the ground he would look up, she down, and their eyes would meet and each would wonder when, if ever, they would look upon one another again. "This was the parting that they had. . . ."

Michal turned back into the bedroom and took an image and some goats' hair and arranged them in David's bed. And when the men who had watched the house for his homecoming and been back to report to Saul that David was now safe in the trap, returned and asked for him she said, "He is sick." So they went back to the palace for further instructions and Michal counted the moments, reckoning the fugitive's progress through the night. And presently the assassins returned again and this time she led them into the bedroom. Another moment gained, and then the inevitable exposure.

She kept her head. David had gone, it was essential for her own well-being to remain on good terms with her father. So she said that David had threatened to kill her unless she aided his escape. And Saul believed her. Anything pointing to David's villainy would be credible to him; besides he trusted Michal. It is a tribute to this woman's skill in the gentle art of sail-trimming that both David, making his way to the mountains and outlawry, and Saul gnawing his fingers with frustrated fury in Gibeah, should equally have had faith in her partisanship.

Some years elapsed before Michal and David met again, and in all that time nothing seemed less likely than that they would ever be united. Michal went back to her father's court, and there news of her fugitive husband would reach her from time to time, for Saul was careful to keep track of his enemy's movements and made many plans for his arrest or murder. The stories that came in were wild and varied. Sometimes David, with his little band of guerrillas, culled from malcontents, and runaway servants, and escaped debtors, was living in caves and hiding places in the hills; sometimes he took service as a mercenary with alien kings who offered him sanctuary and pay.

One can imagine Michal's feelings and the invidiousness of her position in the court of Israel when it became known that David had sold his sword and the swords of the six hundred who followed him to Achish, King of Gath, Israel's hereditary enemy.

Other stories came in too, less shocking to the general public in that age of polygamy, but no more welcome to Michal's ear. David had married again. Presently there were two women with him, Ahinoam a woman of Jezreel, and Abigail the Carmelite. It seemed that David had renounced his nationality and his wife and that Michal would be left to live out her days, years and years of days, as a lonely woman who was neither maid, wife nor widow.

From such a fate her realistic, mundane, ordinary human nature saved her. She may have known her romantic moments when, leaning against a pillar in the background of the throne room, she had listened to a young man singing and playing his harp. But she was not a romantic; and her story is not a fairy tale. She neither pined away from sorrow nor remained steadfastly faithful to her lost love, defying her father when he attempted to make a second marriage for her. Instead she married Phalti, and if she retained any mournful memories, any yearnings for her vanished young harpist, young hero, young husband, she hid them well, for Phalti was very happy with her, as indeed almost any man might have been. For although Michal was ordinary enough, she was intelligent and pliable of mind, a worldly creature, at home in the world and happy in it, capable of setting her sail according to the prevailing wind. Such women are responsible for much of the happiness in the life of men.

Even David, through all these tumultuous and eventful years, had remembered her. He had acquired what for a man in his circumstances was a large harem of women; there were six of them by the time he was acknowledged king of Israel, and each had borne him a son. Yet after the battle of Mount Gilboa and the death of Saul and his son Jonathan, when the adherents of Saul sent Abner to tender their capitulation and pledge their allegiance and ask his mercy, the first thing David said to them was, "Well, I will make a league with thee; but one thing I require of thee, that is—thou shalt not see my face except thou first bring Michal, Saul's daughter."

It was a wonderful compliment. A woman or two may have started a war in the history of the world; Helen, we know, "launched a thousand ships and sacked the topless towers of Ilium," but I can think, offhand, of no other woman whose possession has formed the operative clause in a peace treaty.

Abner and Ishbosheth, Michal's brother, accepted David's terms, and they tore her away from Phalti, who followed her, weeping unashamedly along the road until Abner ordered him back. And then this pair, who had last looked upon each other through the gathering night with a rope dangling and a wall looming between them, came face to face again.

The meeting, after many years, of erstwhile lovers, is never an emotionally simple thing. Romantic stories which pretend that it is so ignore the work of time and affect to believe that during the interval the minds and bodies of the lovers have been in a kind of cold storage from which at the moment of reunion they are able to emerge unchanged. But the fact is otherwise. Experience develops and living changes people, and those who come together after years of absence are not identical with those who had parted. So it was with David and Michal. They had both developed along lines which were already laid down for them when they whispered their tearful farewells through the darkness.

Materially their positions had reversed, too. When they parted he had been a favourite, out of favour, fleeing for his life, with no inch of land to call his own, no house to be his home. And she had been the daughter of the ruling monarch. When they met again David was already king of the greater part of Israel and on the eve of being king of the whole, and she was the daughter of a dead and defeated and disgraced king, and the wife of a nonentity.

But that could have been adjusted. David had remembered Michal even if she had forgotten him; and he owed her his life; and whatever his faults a conventional materialism was not one of them. He had remembered her with love, and now he was prepared to take her back and give her her rightful place as his first wife.

Unfortunately, during those intervening years, they had developed along divergent lines. Michal, never a very spiritually minded woman, had grown hard and conventional. Saul's affection for David was—if we except his superstitious visit to the woman of Endor—the last evidence of his consciousness of the world behind the world, and it is not likely that for Michal's husband he would have chosen a very godly man. Michal had become accustomed to the single-minded devotion of an ordinary human being and now—no longer in her first youth—she was called upon to adjust herself to the very un-ordinary man into whom her talented shepherd boy had grown.

David, on the other hand, although during his exile he had done many things to modern eyes unbecoming in a godly man, had never lost his awareness of the spiritual world or his faith in, and his consciousness of, Jehovah as the moulder of his destiny. The conception of God as a Being invisible and intangible, yet existent and vital and imminent, was still in its infancy, and one sees over and over again in the Old Testament story that a man's conscious acknowledgement of this invisible force is of vastly greater importance than his actual behaviour. (Morally judged, Esau was preferable to Jacob, just as, by all standards of hospitality, centuries later, Martha was preferable to Mary; but in the eyes of Heaven what mattered was the attitude of *mind*.) In this respect David had never failed. He might be bloody and lustful and tricky, but he was these things in the sight of his God. He might take the holy shew-bread from the altar and share it with his hungry horde of mercenaries, but when he did so it was not because he believed that there was nothing behind the altar, but because he was certain, from the moving of the spirit within himself, that what was behind the altar would understand and condone.

For years he had lived in close touch, often in direct communication, with the unseen; and these same years had hardened Michal, who had loved him, into her mould, the ordinary, conventional, worldly minded woman who could make happy almost any man except one of David's type.

Upon the minor, nerve-fraying, destructive differences that were inevitable between them, a pair of lovers too late reunited, history sheds no light. The historian is busy with David's further triumphs and has no time to spare for Michal's bewilderment and muddled memories of a young lover and fitful regrets for Phalti. But their story ends in a noisy clash of personalities. That was inevitable, for Michal, though ordinary enough, was no cipher, and David was God's troubadour.

Soon after their reunion he scored another victory against the Philistines and then went on to turn the Jebusites out of Jerusalem, that strongly fortified, rock-founded city which had defied all former attempts of the Israelites to capture it. It was the obvious future capital of the country and, when it fell, David visualised in it the Great Temple and the Great Palace which were to be for Bathsheba's son to rear. But as a first step he must bring up the Ark of the Covenant and place it with solemn ceremonial upon the spot where he himself intended to build the Temple, and the day when the Ark moved into Jerusalem was incomparably the greatest day that Israel had ever known. Dancing, shouting crowds, hysterical with religious and patriotic fervour, followed the Ark into the captured city, and David, the religious, as well as the civil and military head of the nation, threw himself into the dancing and singing without restraint. He would have done so if he had still been the shepherd boy of Bethlehem, for he was a musician, a poet, immensely susceptible to the significance of a situation. For years Saul had hunted him down as men hunt wild animals, yet when Saul was dead David had taken his harp and composed a song, immortal and haunting in its beauty. "Ye daughters of Israel, weep over Saul who clothed you in scarlet with other delights." If he could feel thus about Saul who was his enemy, how violent must have been his emotion at this coming into the new capital of the Ark of Jehovah who had through all these years guided and favoured and supported him.

Michal, from her privileged place along the line of procession, looked down and saw the man she had loved, the King of Israel, behaving like a drunken man, his clothing disarrayed, his face distorted, dancing and shouting, oblivious to everything in the world save that the Ark, the only earthly manifestation of Israel's God, was coming in triumph into the city which God had given His people. Subject to no such spiritual afflatus herself she looked at him dispassionately and thought that he looked like a drunken clown. Any observer to another person's complete abandon feels the same, especially if the abandon arises from an intoxication which the observer has never known. And Michal had never been religiously drunk. To her earth-bound eyes the Ark was just a little wooden structure being borne on two poles; and David's transport of emotion an hysterical, shocking lapse from dignity.

There may have been eyes as blind, hearts as unmoved, as hers in Jerusalem that day; but their possessors refrained from speech. Michal, however, as soon as the ceremony was ended and David had returned home in a state of happy exhaustion, spoke her mind. The words were few, but they had venom, and pungency, and were full of the wish to hurt. "How glorious," she said, "was the king of Israel, today, who uncovered himself in the eyes of the handmaidens of his servants as one of the vain fellows uncovereth himself." It was all there—her shame for him, her utter lack of understanding, the blow which her respect for him had sustained. One can even see the hint that she, daughter of a king, had a better notion than he, the upstart, of how a king should behave. But the barbed speech proves too that she was not, even now, indifferent to him. No woman feels shame for, or wishes to hurt, the man in whom she is no longer interested.

Other men have suffered bitter criticism from their wives and either borne it with fortitude or ignored it. But, for David, Michal had trodden on holy ground. His answer to her was simple. "It was before the Lord which chose me before thy father and before his house to appoint me ruler over Israel." And he added, with truth (for we remember Uriah), that he would do worse things, vile things, things that would make him base in his own sight.

That was the end between them. David never looked upon her as his wife again. The Old Testament says that that worst fate for a Jewish woman befell her—she bore no children to the day of her death. Josephus says that she returned to Phalti and bore him five children.

Looking back to the story's beginning, when a young princess fell in love with a handsome young shepherd to the strains of the music of a harp, who shall say which is the sadder ending?

Chapter 12

BATHSHEBA

AUTHORIZED VERSION: II *Samuel 11*—I *Kings 2*

"They gave me a little beauty, and a man used it
as a screen to hide the love he dared not know,
a love of God, but the love of man confused it . . ."
(*Humbert Wolfe*: REQUIEM)

Of all the women in the Old Testament, important enough to be named and described, Bathsheba comes nearest to being a nonentity. So far as we can see from her story she never performed a single action under the thrust of her own impulse, never uttered a word which was not previously put into her mouth by some man. Yet she was the mother of Solomon; she was instrumental in obtaining the throne for him; because of her the Temple at Jerusalem bore Solomon's name, not David's; and she brought death to two men. And all this she achieved by being beautiful and pliant and obedient. These are supposedly female virtues, and Bathsheba possessed them in such measure that she is as typical of one kind of woman as the queen of Sheba is of another.

Her story is brief enough, and—even when allowances are made for differences in time and place—a little distasteful.

She was the wife of Uriah the Hittite who was one of David's soldiers, a particular, faithful soldier who, when the story opens, was away at the war which the King of Israel was waging against the Ammonites. David, for once, was not in the field with his army, but had entrusted the campaign to Joab while he himself lingered in Jerusalem. David, who had a many-sided nature, may have had his fill of fighting, or a malignant fate may have been at work, spinning out the doom of David, the prelude to Solomon and the immortality of a woman who was beautiful and nothing else. For while the army camped before the walls of Rabbah and Uriah lay out in the fields, David, walking the roof of his palace in the cool of evening, saw from that place of vantage a woman washing herself, and she was "very beautiful to look upon."

For David, the shepherd-harpist, the soldier-poet, the father whose cry, "Oh Absalom, my son, my son," has rung down the echoing corridors of time, God Himself was prepared to make certain allowances. David was capable of that supreme abandon to the emotion of the moment that is one of the marks, and curses, of the artistic temperament. David, when he was hungry, had snatched the holy shew-bread from Jehovah's altar; David, when he was jubilant over the Ark's entry into Jerusalem had behaved as though he were intoxicated and so revolted and alienated one of the women who had loved him. And now, with all the vigour and passion of his violent poetic nature he looked upon Bathsheba and desired her.

He made some inquiries about her and discovered that she was called Bathsheba and was the wife of Uriah the Hittite; a married woman, rightfully immune from any man's lust.

But David was King of Israel. In a short time, by a series of almost miraculous happenings, he had been raised from his position as the youngest son of an obscure sheep farmer to be the ruler of twelve expanding tribes. God had been with him; he had never lost a battle or failed in a venture. Saul and Saul's son and Saul's daughter had been the victims of his personal charm; his enemies had been chaff for his winnowing. Jerusalem, that rock-founded city which had defied all his predecessors, had fallen to him, and there established in it was his new house of cedar and the Ark of the Covenant between its curtains which he intended soon to replace by marble. Everything that he had ever wanted or aspired to had come to him. He was the spoilt child of God. And what was Bathsheba but one more toy, hotly coveted, easily acquired, soon laid aside?

He sent for her and she came. Not, one feels because he was King of Israel or because she was flattered by his attention. Later on she took an order from Nathan and later still a request from Adonijah with that same unquestioning, unprotesting compliance, obedient as a dog though less faithful, for a dog might have remembered Uriah.

The poet, the artist in David, no doubt waited eagerly for her coming; the man had his way with her, and then she returned to her house, and that, very easily, might have been the end of the matter. Her beauty was of the kind that rouses nothing but an easily sated lust. David had no desire for her company or for further association with her. The thing was ended and she could go back to her house and await Uriah's return.

But that casual union had proved fruitful and before long Bathsheba—so typically feminine in her compliance and her trust—sent to David to say that she was with child. Her message to him is actually reported verbatim, immensely simple, with no hint of panic, no suggestion of self-reliance. "I am with child," that was the wording, with, behind the words, the whole enormous pressure of the female fertilised—what are you going to do about it? You are the person responsible. You must act.

One must admire the frankness and matter-of-factness of the Old Testament narrative; it deals with this timeless situation in a manner that makes it contemporary after thousands of years. An attractive woman has conceived a child while her husband is away at the war; dates all awry; neighbours counting their fingers; Uriah remembering when he was last home.

David, with the craftiness and guilefulness which are often the ugly accompaniments of his kind of temperament, sent to Joab requesting that Uriah should be sent back to report the progress of the war. When he arrived the king spent some time discussing the campaign with him, and no doubt some of his questions were eager and genuine, for by this time the war against Ammon would rank fully equal with Bathsheba in his mind. And Uriah would be flattered that he had been chosen to make the report, and would see nothing but kindness in his king's dismissal at the end of the interview, "Go down to thy house . . ." As soon as the soldier had left the throne room David ordered that "a mess of meat," the ingredients for a reunion feast, should be despatched to Uriah's house, and it is safe to deduce that he spent the evening in a mood of self-congratulation over an awkward corner safely rounded and a scandal averted. Mingled with his complacence would be the tolerant thought (not in the least jealous) of Bathsheba and Uriah making merry over the wine and the bakemeats he had provided and then going to their connubial bed; and mingled with such thoughts would be practical military broodings over the facts which Uriah had presented. So far as David was concerned the story of Bathsheba was told, the incident closed.

But Uriah unfortunately for himself was a conscientious soldier. When he was dismissed he went and lay down in the guardroom with the other soldiers and made no attempt to go to his own house or to visit his wife. There is portrayed the fate of the beautiful nonentities; David, who had been her lover could calmly contemplate her husband in full possession; Uriah, her husband, could come within walking distance of her and allow her to remain unaware of his presence.

Somebody with a full and cynical knowledge of the situation told David in the morning, greasy eyed, tongue in cheek. What now? David sent for Uriah and reasoned with him and received an answer which at any other moment would have moved the poet to tears. Uriah said that while other men were at camp "in the open fields" he did not feel justified in going home to his own house and his own wife simply because he had chanced to be called to make a report in the capital.

Was it a scrupulous integrity, an almost incredible conscientiousness, or had a tongue come out of a cheek in order to drop poison into Uriah's ear? No one now can tell. There was in the palace someone who knew. Someone who had told the name of the woman, someone who had thought Uriah's night in the guardroom worthy of report. Had that somebody whispered? But even if he had, Uriah's attitude is the measure of Bathsheba's failure. Any man who cared a jot for her would have gone hotfoot down to that house, full of questions and recriminations.

But it is possible that Uriah's integrity was unstained by guile. His refusal to go to his house may have been the outcome of an overdeveloped sense of duty and it may, to a degree, mitigate Bathsheba's easy acceptance of a lover. Had she seen him put duty before love in time past?

Whatever the reason for Uriah's behaviour he was sealing his own doom. David gave him another chance. He asked him to stay in Jerusalem for another twenty-four hours and that night invited him to supper and made him drunk. The idea that alcohol tends to loosen inhibitions and to paralyse one's highest faculties had not then been evolved as a theory, but David would know from experience that a drunken man would be likely to set his desire before his sense of duty. But drunkenness also tends to reveal what is real and fundamental in a man, and Uriah drunk was still a soldier. He may have reeled away from his king's supper table, but he reeled back to the guardroom and lay down amongst his fellow soldiers and David was left to face the fact that so far as policy was concerned Uriah's visit to Jerusalem had been utterly wasted.

And meanwhile Bathsheba sat in her house with the pleasant, pathological lethargy of early pregnancy superimposed upon her normal placidity, and doubtless she accepted the "mess of meat" which had been so differently intentioned as a sign that David was interested in her well-being and active in her interest.

Up in his house of cedar David mused, grew impatient, even a little frightened. Enormous licence was allowed to men in those days, especially to kings; but there was something sacrosanct about marriage; even Pharaoh had turned Sarah out of his harem as soon as he discovered that she was married to Abraham; and the prospect of being convicted of an adulterous association with the wife of one of his own soldiers while that soldier was away fighting Israel's war was a prospect that daunted even David. He had done his best to find a happy solution to the problem and had failed. What now?

It is a little sad to think that had Uriah been a trifle less obdurate, or Bathsheba's hold on him a little stronger, his leave might have been prolonged until the Ammonites were defeated and they might have lived out their days together, with a child who showed a poetry and a passion which would have astounded all who knew his parents.

But then, what of Solomon? Did this beautiful nonentity bear, hidden within her, some quality which alone she possessed and which, allied to some quality in David, would result in the production of the wisest man of all time? Must Uriah die and David be cast from God's favour and Bathsheba promoted to the palace harem, all in order that Solomon might be what he was?

Uriah must die; that at least was certain. David had decided that, before the night was out; and when in the morning Uriah returned to the army he carried with him a letter to Joab containing a frank, unequivocal order, "Set ye Uriah in the fore front of the hottest battle and retire ye from him, that he may be smitten and die."

And the tragic thing is that this order was written by the man whose harp music had been capable of exorcising Saul's evil spirit; by the boy who had faced Goliath with a sling, by the child who, intrepid in the defence of a flock of senseless sheep, had slain a lion and a bear. "All power corrupts, and absolute power corrupts absolutely." Of no man was that sorry saying more true than of David.

But it is possible to overpity Uriah. His name has come down to us as the name of the betrayed and the doomed. But whether he slept in that guardroom out of suspicion or out of integrity at least he went back to his place at the front with the satisfaction of knowing that he had acted as he had wished to act; and he did not know the contents of that fatal letter; and he took his place in the hottest part of the battle with pride knowing that that was where "the valiant men were." If greasy-eyes, tongue-in-cheek *had* whispered, of which we have no proof, Uriah may have had suspicions of his wife, but of his captain, who, by his own behaviour he had shown to be of more importance than a merely beautiful woman, he had no doubt at all. He was a soldier and he went to his death fighting for Israel in the company of valiant men. Not a pitiable fate.

But David had "displeased the Lord." He had acted cruelly,

from a mean and conventional motive. Jehovah was very tolerant with David, whatever his antics, at a certain level; when he dropped into pettiness and ordinariness he must be judged by ordinary standards. The harvest of his God's displeasure would ripen, would be reaped to the last ear.

Outwardly all was well. Even for Joab who had the unpleasant duty of reporting that the attack upon Rabbah had been unsuccessful. One of his men had been killed by a piece of millstone hurled from the city walls by a woman, and Joab rather feared that David might ask why the attack had not been made with more subtlety. But the messenger who carried the report was instructed to say that Uriah the Hittite was amongst the slain, and Joab, remembering a certain letter, imagined that the king's attention would be distracted by this apparently irrelevant piece of information.

Bathsheba, compliant, unquestioning, breeding female, received the news and performed the perfunctory days of mourning and then, summoned by David, went up to the women's quarters of the house of cedar and there, in privacy, bore, in due time, her son.

This was not Solomon; this was the foredoomed, nameless "child" who must die because of his father's sin. Nathan the prophet predicted his death when he came to rebuke David by telling him the touching story of the man who had but one ewe lamb which the rich man stole in order to feed "the wayfaring man." (If a better analogy for a passing lust of the eye has ever been voiced it has escaped my notice!) The story moved the ordinarily warm-hearted David to violent threats of vengeance, which in turn evoked the damning, immortal sentence, "Thou art the man."

So the child of Bathsheba sickened, and David lay on the bare earth and fasted and prayed to God to spare him. But Nathan's prophecy was not to be mocked, and the child died. David, once more at the mercy of his mercurial temperament, rose from the ground, washed, changed his clothes and went into the house of God to worship, and then returned to his own house and sat down to eat. Some of his attendants voiced their wonder at such behaviour; while the child lived they said, he had fasted and mourned, now, when it was dead he seemed almost to rejoice. David replied with one of his apt, telling speeches, "Now he is dead wherefore should I fast? Can I bring him back? I shall go to him, but he shall not return to me."

There was one thing more to do. Bathsheba, the bereaved mother, must be comforted, and having eaten and rationalised his own grief David went to her. And once again he saw that she was beautiful. They did not know, these smitten sinners weeping over their dead child, that they were beating out the path for Solomon, measuring out the rhythm for the Song of Songs; but out of their shared grief they struck an echoing note of an old brief passion and that was sufficient. Bathsheba conceived again, and this time the child was Solomon.

After that Bathsheba disappears behind the harem curtains like a beautiful puppet temporarily laid away. She was not the first wife, nor the favourite wife, nor even the mother of David's favourite son. It is open to question whether her mind was even capable of the wistful reflection, the wonder whether her life might not have been fuller and brighter as Uriah's "one ewe lamb" than as one of the wives and concubines of a man whose days were darkening with trouble and whose mind was occupied with concerns far apart from the scented softnesses of his harem.

For, for David the halcyon days of God's favour were ended. Nathan had said that, because he had slain Uriah with the sword of the children of Ammon, the sword should never depart from his house and the prophecy was being fulfilled. The sword had been unscabbarded by Absalom, the best loved of his sons. "The storied prince with wondrous hair that won men's hearts and wrought his bale," had risen up in rebellion against his father, and David was forced into a reluctant, half-hearted war against his own favourite. Did he ever remember, as he waged a war in which at the end of each battle he must ask, "Is the young man Absalom safe?" that he himself had once been a favourite with Saul?

Absalom, caught up by the hair in an oak tree, was stabbed to the heart by Joab, the same captain who had set Uriah in the forefront of the battle and who was still serving David to the best of his ability; and Bathsheba and the rest of David's women had little good of the heart-broken man who was crying, "Would God I had died for thee, oh Absalom, my son."

Nor was the full vengeance for Uriah's death taken then. David, who had set his heart upon building a temple to house the Ark, was forbidden to attempt the task because he was "A man of blood." Whose blood? His wars had been waged against Jehovah's enemies, the heathen tribes whose destruction was necessary to Hebrew survival. The people had sung, "Saul hath slain his thousands and David his ten thousands," and there had been no hint of God's distaste for that blood-spilling. Nor was it the blood of Goliath of Gath that cried from the ground and made David unfit to build the holy temple. It was the blood of Uriah the Hittite which had been shed, not because David desired his wife, but because he wanted to avert a scandal. God could forgive in his favourite a defiance of all laws, but he could not forgive a petty, wriggling subterfuge.

So, in waning favour and with troubles gathering about him, David the musician, the poet, the lover, grew old; so old and cold and moribund that even Abishag, the pretty little Shunammite virgin whom they found to attend him, could rouse no vestige of the old fire within his blood. But he was so long in dying that Adonijah, dead Absalom's brother, grew impatient and set himself up as king, seducing men of influence with the promise of important offices, and the common people with feasts of sheep and fat cattle.

And here, for a moment, Bathsheba emerges again, to play her little foreordained part, make her little dictated speech and wield her enormous, disproportionate influence.

Nathan, the prophet, had not been "bought" by Adonijah; he was still David's man; and activated by jealousy, or inspiration, hatred of Adonijah or from something that his prophetic eye had detected in Bathsheba's son, he determined to make a bid for the throne for Solomon. So he sought out Bathsheba and told her to go into the room where David lay dying and to reproach him in that, having promised the throne to her son, he had done nothing positive towards establishing him upon it. In the course of his speech he calls Adonijah "the son of Haggith"—and an aroma of old, bitter jealousies stirs from the phrase; for Haggith was also the mother of Absalom.

Bathsheba, who years before had come up from Uriah's house at the king's word, and gone down again, and sent her little trusting message, and waited, and heard of her husband's death, and performed her days of mourning and then entered the palace for good, now went obediently into the room where David lay, cold under the heaped clothes, unresponsive to the young Shunammite whose virginity was still unassailed.

Did any memories stir then? Of a warm scented night when this sluggish blood was hot with desire; of stolen sweetness; of pleasure sharpened by a sense of guilt. Or did the ghost of Uriah move in the shadows, unforgiving, mocking because "the end of might . . . is death at last." We only know that Bathsheba said precisely what she had been told to say and that her words waked, for a moment in the dying man, the old wild spirit which had made David face the lion and the bear, defy Goliath of Gath, defy Saul the king, and, in the final issue, where this now middle-aged, complaining woman was concerned, defy God Himself. He was old and he was dying, but he was still king of Israel.

From his bed he gave exact and detailed instructions for the appointment of Solomon as his successor, even stipulating that Solomon should be set on his own mule. Then, after a final interview with the young man who was to succeed him, David died.

Even then Bathsheba had not spoken the last of her set, fateful lines. Solomon forgave Adonijah his attempt to forestall him and Adonijah accepted the new situation philosophically. He only wanted one thing, and that was Abishag, the little Shunammite, for his wife. So he decided to give Bathsheba a line to speak. He sought an interview of her and this strange woman, with no more loyalty to her son than she had had to her husband, received him, pleasantly. She *must* have known that, considering the circumstances, Adonijah was asking a dangerous thing. She must have known that a dead king's possessions were the heritage of his successor and that Adonijah would for years live under the cloud of attempted usurpation. But her contribution to their conversation consists of the words, "Say on," and again "Say on," and finally, "Well, I will speak for thee unto the king." The whole of the woman, the whole of her placid, compliant, unperceptive puppet nature is there revealed.

But, again, she was handling dynamite as though it were dough. She went in to Solomon with her request, saying, "I have a small petition . . ." It seemed so to her. She was, no doubt, very much surprised when her son said venomously, "Ask for him the kingdom also." The irony of that must have been made very obvious; for Bathsheba would do what any man ordered yet she refrained from asking the kingdom for Adonijah.

But she had done harm enough. Solomon, sensing his half-brother's presumption ordered him to be killed. So the blood of two men stains the hands of Bathsheba, the puppet, who never did anything except by some man's order. More deadly than Jael, more fatal than Delilah, this nonentity who was "beautiful to look upon."

Chapter 13

THE WOMAN OF EN-DOR

AUTHORIZED VERSION: I *Samuel* 28:3-25

"Oh, the road to En-dor is the oldest road
And the craziest road of all.
Straight it runs to the Witch's abode
As it did in the days of Saul.
And nothing has changed of the sorrow in store
For such as go down on the road to En-dor."

(*Kipling*: ROAD TO EN-DOR)

She is so well-known, so often referred to by this title that it is a little startling to realise that never once during the bible narrative is the word "witch" used: and one remembers that the Authorised Version was compiled during the reign of James I when witch hunting was reaching a peak of frenzy, and imagine one of the compilers, influenced, perhaps unconsciously, by the gossip of his day, sitting down and writing the subtitle of her story, "Saul seeketh a witch." But at the heart of all the concepts of witchcraft lay the idea of a compact, a contract, a traffic with the devil, and there is no hint of that in the story of the Woman of En-dor, as the Bible calls her. Hers is the story of a medium who on one notable occasion conducted a successful séance. And the Bible, in many ways the most catholic and tolerant of histories, simply tells her story and leaves it without comment. What makes it remarkable is that in this one woman, with her familiar spirit, all women of her kind are portrayed, pin-pointed forever.

She was by trade a medium and once a king resorted to her. That is her story. That king was Saul, the first king of Israel, who had at one time been the recipient of divine favour but who had proved himself a materialist at heart and had been abandoned by his God.

The story of Saul—strictly speaking outside the scope of this book—is one of the saddest extant. He had disobeyed Jehovah's orders with regard to the property of the Amalekites and it really does read as though his greed for possession over a number of cattle and asses led to his downfall. For years he had been the victim of a mental affliction, an immense, incurable depression, and now, when his days were literally numbered, he had upon the one hand domestic war against David, whom he had loved and promoted, and upon the other a war against the Philistines, the traditional enemies of Israel.

In the past Saul had had the prophet Samuel as guide and mentor. Samuel seldom spoke him a comfortable word, often rebuked him, never praised him, but he had been there, the seer, the very voice of God. But now Samuel was dead. All Israel had lamented him and he had been buried, with every conceivable honour, in his own city of Ramah. And Saul, who had no mental or spiritual resources of his own, was left alone.

Even the "unco' guid" can hardly withhold a measure of pity from Saul. If tragedy be indeed what the Greeks held it—the conflict of man with the gods—then Saul is, of all men, a tragic figure. He tried, he tried very hard, to establish some means of contact with the Almighty. In his extremity "he inquired of the Lord, the Lord answered him not, neither by dreams, nor by the prophets." He had been materialistic and he was to reap the materialist's bitter harvest: for him there was no voice, nor any that answered.

But there was that final road of despair. There was the woman of En-dor. And the dramatic thing is that if Saul had fully had his way in the past this woman would have been dead some time ago. For Saul himself had taken pains to put away all wizards and all those who had familiar spirits. So now, when the open road to guidance was closed to him—Samuel being dead and the other prophets useless—it looked for a moment as though the dark bye-road which he was tempted to take was also barred.

But Saul appealed to his servants and presently one of them produced the information that there was a woman with a familiar spirit living at En-dor.

Nothing is explicitly told us about this woman, one of the lonely survivors of the purge; but it is safe to judge that she was either extremely crafty and cautious, or very popular with her neighbours, or so immensely feared that no one had dared expose her. All three reasons are indicated in the text itself. She was very careful when Saul first approached her; she later proved to be generous and kindly, which would make for popularity; and she had a genuine supernatural power which would make her feared. By her carefulness, or her kindness, or her dread ability, she had survived and was there, in the hour of Saul's need, in her house at En-dor. And, by one of those felicitous chances which occur now and then in literature, the very name of her place of dwelling has a dark, sinister sound, a dark, ominous look. If it had been the Battle of En-dor it would have been a lost battle; if it had been the Palace of En-dor it would have been crumbling to ruin. As it is the house at En-dor is touched by the murk of hell, shadowy with ghosts, dark with the knowledge of what should not be known. And yet the woman who lived in it, was, apart from her dreadful power, normal, hospitable, kindly.

Saul took the road to En-dor by night, disguised, wearing unkingly raiment and taking with him two companions whom he could trust. It would not be a cheerful journey, for added to the king's ordinary profound depression would be anxiety about the immediate future and the knowledge that in making this visit he was denying one of his convictions. In happier days he had been the enemy of the "familiar spirits," and now, in despair, he was seeking a service of them.

The woman opened the door of her low small house. We know that it was small, for there was no place for the king to sit, even when his royalty had been discovered, but the woman's own bed; and we know that she lived in squalor, for there is mention of a calf being "in the house" with her. Even to her domestic circumstances she adheres to type, for the prosperous witch of old time, the prosperous medium of ours, is so exceptional as to be an anomaly.

She did not see through Saul's disguise, and that fact is very significant. Ordinarily she was as blind and as easily deceived as any other creature. And as Saul greeted her and told her what he wanted of her he may have thought, with sick longing, of Samuel, whose seer's eye no disguise would have baffled for a moment.

The woman of En-dor listened to his request and then made her careful answer. Saul, she said, had put away all those who had a familiar spirit, and she suspected her visitors of being his agents, seeking to lay a snare for her life. But she did not deny that she had a familiar spirit, nor did she say that these visitors by night were asking the impossible of her. The first requirement for any sort of achievement was hers—she believed in herself and in her own power.

Saul assured her that no ill should result from her acceding to his request, and even this assurance, with its suggestion of great power behind it, did not open her eyes to his identity. But it was enough to persuade her. She asked, "Whom shall I bring up unto thee?" and there is a suggestion of great power behind that question, too; as though she had command of all the dead. Saul said, "Bring me up Samuel."

The historian, to whom all this is only a prelude to the battle of Mount Gilboa, cheats a little here; he hastens on, and we shall never know in what manner this, the first recorded séance, was conducted. What spell did she weave? What rites did she perform? Who, or what, was that familiar spirit? The two so common to our day, the young Red Indian and the old Egyptian priest, would not, I feel, figure here, for the woman of En-dor had never heard of North America and Egyptian priests would be to her as common and mundane as French politicians to us.

But Samuel came to her call; she saw him and recognised him; and she cried in a loud voice. Was it a cry of recognition, or of vast, horrified astonishment? And as soon as she saw Samuel she recognised Saul, as though something emanating from the seer's personality had illumined her blindness. Saul saw nothing. He heard the woman cry out and asked her what she saw and she told him, "An old man cometh up: and he is covered with a mantle." Then Saul was satisfied that he was in the presence of the dead, and when he had bowed himself to the ground he explained his plight and asked for advice.

This spirit, roughly summoned back to earth, was recognisable as Samuel, just as Moses and Elias—we are told—were recognisable to the two disciples upon the Mount of Transfiguration: and the voice which emerged from the shadows was the voice of Samuel; and the words it spoke were as minatory and comfortless as any the prophet had ever spoken to the king in his lifetime. He foretold the battle of Mount Gilboa which was to take place next day and which was to be immortalised by David's lament for Jonathan; he told Saul what the result of that battle would be; —"Tomorrow shalt thou and thy sons be with me." Saul who had made that journey through the dark to dabble in a thing which he had himself forbidden, knew that the last desperate hope was gone. Even Samuel, summoned from the dead, had no comfortable thing to say, no counsel to offer. The voice which had so often irked Saul in the past, yet which was of all voices the one which he had longed to hear again, had only words of doom to speak, only defeat and death to prophesy. As soon as its message was delivered it fell back into silence, and Saul collapsed so that he lay "all along the earth."

It was then that the woman of En-dor displayed both her essential femininity and the goodness of her heart. The offer of physical comfort for a spiritual woe is one of the most characteristic things about women. There is, literally, no sorrow so deep, no horror so appalling that some woman, somewhere, will not attempt to counteract with the offer of a cup of tea. Tea was unknown to the woman of En-dor, but she offered its equal. Coming to the distraught king, where he lay on the floor, she said that she had done what he asked and in return he must do what she requested, eat a morsel of bread in order that he might have strength.

The offer of the "morsel of bread" was the automatic female reaction to the sight of anyone in trouble; but what the woman did later on is proof of a generous, forgiving and unself-seeking nature. For presently Saul rose from the floor and sat on the bed and accepted her offer of refreshment. And then she did not content herself with bringing the "morsel of bread." She killed and dressed and cooked the calf which was in the house with her, and she made and baked new bread, providing the best feast that it was in her power to give. And all this for the king who, in the days of his power, had been her enemy and the enemy of all like her; all this for the man whose doom she had just heard pronounced, the man who by this time tomorrow would be dead, incapable of showing, or returning, any favour. By some standards this woman of En-dor was an evil woman, a dabbler in magic, a creature outside the pale of safe normality, but she acted—hundreds of years before the words were spoken—upon the dictum of Christ, who said that good should be done to those who could not return it again.

When the meal, macabre as any ever taken in a death cell, akin, over the centuries, to that wedding feast of Hitler and Eva Braun before their suicide, was done, Saul and his companions went away into the night. If this were Saul's story one might speculate upon his state of mind as he walked away to face what he knew must happen tomorrow, and one might salute the courage which had enabled him to take his share of that impromptu feast. There is there some echo of the "goodly young man" who had been chosen to be king of Israel and who had been anointed by Samuel.

But this is the story of the woman of En-dor. Is it safe to say that she closed her door after her visitors, sighed a little, cleared away her dishes and went back to her bed?

What is safe to say is that her story, brief and incomplete as it is, throws a little light in a dark place. It admits, and it condemns, the thing which we now call "spiritualism." Samuel was a revered and honoured character in Israel; no serious historian would, for the sake of making a dramatic story, have taken liberties even with his ghost. And this story clearly states that in response to some compulsion which this woman could exercise, Samuel appeared, physically recognisable, and audible. The most ardent spiritualist could not ask for more. That is the admission. The condemnation lies in the first words which Samuel's ghost addressed to Saul—and he said it to Saul, the inquirer, not to the woman, the medium. "Why hast thou disquieted me, to bring me up?" The sentence hardly bears thinking about. Samuel had been a good man, he had served God from his youth up. He had died; and the fact that this kindly, hospitable woman had by some means the power to disquiet him after his death postulates the existence of another power, an immensely potent power directly opposed to that of God. The Bible, of course, never hesitates to admit the existence, or the power, of the devil; and the devil, although he is not mentioned, lurks upon the fringe of this story. Only upon the fringe, however. For Samuel, although disquieted, was still himself; and the woman, it is obvious, had not been entirely corrupted. That calf was as much an offering to God as it would have been if it had gone up to the altar and had its throat slit by a priest.

Chapter 14

A NAMELESS WOMAN

AUTHORIZED VERSION: I *Kings 3:16-28*

"A mother in Israel."
(*Book of Judges 5:7*)

The wisdom of Solomon, third king of Israel, had become a legend even during his lifetime. After his death it passed into a by-word, so that people still say, "As wise as Solomon." It is written that in the very early days of his reign he had a dream in which God appeared to him and said, "Ask what I shall give thee," and Solomon, with that humility of mind which is itself one of the roots of wisdom, replied, "I am but a little child . . . give therefore thy servant an understanding heart . . . that I may discern between good and evil." And God gave him wisdom, and promised that all the other things, for which he might have asked and refrained, should be added as well.

So in an age, and a region, when little was asked of a king save that he should be a good leader in battle and an imposing figure on public occasions, Israel was ruled for one glittering span of years by a man of intellect and rare maturity of mind. Over the natural talent for poetry, which he had inherited from David his father, was laid a patina of discernment, balanced judgement and insight, so unusual in that generation that the Queen of Sheba undertook a long and arduous journey to see for herself whether such phenomenal wisdom really existed or not; and kings from neighbouring countries sent him their problems to solve.

In one of the stories told about him, there is embedded a little portrait, so slight, so delicate, so apparently unimportant, that the woman who is portrayed in it is not even named. She shines for a moment, a mere globule of foam in the wake of the glittering legend of Solomon, and then vanishes.

But hers is no reflected light; she has a strong vibrant existence of her own; and as a study of one aspect of womanhood she repays attention since she stands for something so fundamental and enduring that she redeems a sordid little story and makes it the best-known, most often quoted example of the great king's wisdom. Nameless—just "a certain woman," or "a harlot," she enjoyed some fame in her own day, for the story spread far and wide, and probably reached the ear of the Queen of Sheba in her far country.

The historian, bent upon the rapid assembling of evidence of Solomon's wisdom, tosses off the story in a few lines. There were, we read, two women who, after the simple, democratic manner of the day, came into Solomon's court in search of justice. They were both harlots and they shared a single room. They had both become pregnant at about the same time, and had borne their children within days of one another. Josephus says that the children were born on the same day, but the Authorised Version, with its three days' difference is preferable, for the plaintiff in the case, telling her story says that there was no witness as they two were alone in the house. The three days' lapse would permit of each helping the other at the critical moment.

One of the babies, sleeping beside his mother, was overlaid by her in the night, and died. The woman who brought the complaint swore that the mother of the dead child had then risen and changed the dead baby for her living one, which she now persisted in retaining. She had waked to find a dead child in her arms, "but when I considered it in the morning, behold it was not my son, which I did bear."

Not a very pretty problem for the King of Israel, the author of the Song of Songs, to consider. There were the two vociferous prostitutes, and the two tiny bastards, one alive and warm, lightly breathing within his swaddling clothes, the other still and dead, hardly more substantial than an autumn leaf. But Solomon gave it his full attention. A point of law—without any known precedent—was involved, and Solomon, legal successor to the old Judges of Israel, was anxious to deal out justice. Also the matter presented a real puzzle, and Solomon was fond of puzzles, he spent hours in inventing them for other people to solve, and hours in solving other people's.

The story makes it quite clear that there was nothing, superficially, to distinguish one woman from the other, to lend credence to one story and to discredit the other. Two women of the same trade who had lived in amity and close proximity in time past would look very much alike. There they were, in the gaudy apparel of their trade, their faces raddled, their hair oiled, the gold coins which they had saved against an evil day dangling against their foreheads and at their wrists. They were both hard, bold women whom life had coarsened; they pursued their quarrel wholeheartedly, contradicting one another even in the presence of the king. To neither eye nor ear was offered one sign to say which was lying and which speaking truthfully. Even the avid eagerness, with which, their story told, they awaited his verdict, their kohl-blackened eyes fixed upon his face, was common to both.

Yet there was the living child, and the dead one; and there were the two women, the one holding her treasure to her breast with every gesture of maternal affection, the other bearing her burden with an air of repudiation. And Solomon knew that his decision would not be concerned with the mere satisfaction of one woman's maternal instinct and the disappointment of the other's; the fate of one woman in the years ahead was involved. For a son was a precious thing even to a harlot. Possession of a baby now meant a roof and a seat by the fire and food in the bowl in those later years when her sorry trade was closed to her and age came on. And one was the living child's mother; the other was not. How to decide?

Solomon considered for a while and then said, "Bring me a sword." The order bewildered everyone. What was he about to do? Perform some magical rite, perhaps, remembered from the old heathen days, some primitive method of trial by ordeal to search out truth and expose the liar. Or had he, by some uncanny method, already detected the liar and sent for the sword to strike her down?

They waited. When the sword came the king made no move to take it; instead he said simply, "Divide the living child in two and give half to one, and half to the other." There is a version of the story which says that he also ordered the dead child to be shared between them—a macabre, but not incredible addition.

And now the bright cold blade of steel has done its work, not upon the soft baby mass of flesh and bone, but upon the knotted problem, and upon the hearts of two women. Truth falls to one side, falsity to the other; the division is straight and plain. Here on the one side is the genuine mother's heart beating in a harlot's bosom, and there upon the other the hard greedy harlot's heart beating in the bosom of the bereaved mother.

Solomon, watching their faces would now see how they differed, would hardly need to wait for their lips to utter. Upon the face of the woman whose child was dead already, although she clutched the living one, there was a sly triumph; an expression which said—at least, if I have lost my son, she will be in the same case; I shall not have the torment of watching her happy with her baby. Upon the face of the mother of the living child there would be the horror and anguish of the woman who sees harm threaten the flesh she bore, death shadow the life she gave. Better, oh better a thousand times that the child should live, even if she never saw or touched it again. Let it live, even though it grew up to call this greedy heartless liar "mother."

Across the pitiful little bundle which was the dead child the mother of the living one cried from her heart, "O my Lord, give her the living child, and in no wise slay it." Over the head of the living child sounded the voice of jealousy and spite, "Let it be neither mine nor thine but divide it."

The puzzle had resolved itself. It was easy for Solomon to raise a finger and say, "She is the mother."

So they gave the little warm bundle into the arms of the woman to whom it belonged. Fortunate child to have escaped being reared by the woman who could have borne to see it sawn in sunder, the woman whose only reason for claiming it must have been the hope of profiting from it. And tears of joy in repossession and relief at tension relaxed fell from the kohl-smeared eyes as the woman hurried out of Solomon's court. One hopes that she reared him successfully and that he was a support and his children a comfort to her when age closed the oldest profession to her.

The story astonished Israel and all without Israel's bounds who heard of it. And Solomon, the possessor of the understanding heart which we now call a knowledge of psychology, probably smiled into his beard, thinking how simple the thing had really been.

He turned his mind to greater matters; he built his great temple and his great palace. He married the daughter of the Pharaoh and took to himself innumerable other women as well; he was intermittently unfaithful to the God who had given him his gift of insight; he became in time a tyrant, for it was his son who uttered the dictum, "My father made your yoke heavy, and I will add to your yoke; my father also chastised you with whips, but I will chastise you with scorpions." It may well have been that Solomon, building up his legend, busy with his architecture and his women and his tyranny, completely forgot the gaudy, noisy prostitute who had once appealed to him for justice. But amongst the proverbs which he penned, there is one, "Love covereth all sins," and perhaps as he wrote it there stirred in his mind the memory of tears springing to hard eyes and flooding over on to raddled cheeks and a hoarse voice crying, "Give her the living child, and in no wise slay it." For a love that is willing to reliquish its object for the object's good is love indeed, and Solomon would be wise enough to remember his encounter with it.

Chapter 15

THE QUEEN OF SHEBA

AUTHORIZED VERSION: I *Kings 10:1-13*

"There is no comfort in the sensual world
For those, who, seeking fire, are brought to heel
By answered questions."

(*Elizabeth Bibesco*: SONNET)

At the beginning of the tenth chapter of the first Book of Kings there are thirteen comparatively short sentences which relate as undecorated, unromantic a story as any in the world, yet it is doubtful whether any similar amount of flat reporting in the whole history of time has ever given rise to so many legends, by-words, imaginative speculations.

Solomon was a great king; he built a great Temple for his God and a great palace for himself in Jerusalem: he had a reputation for wisdom. And one of his fellow monarchs—a woman—was curious enough about him, his buildings and his wisdom to make a long journey in order to visit him. She was satisfied that reports had not exaggerated anything; she gave him presents and received presents in return and went back to her own country. Surely one of the simplest stories ever written. One suspects that its very simplicity is responsible for its fertility. There must, said the later historians, have been more in it than that; and so the legends began.

In the first place there was a mystery about the woman and the country she ruled. The Old Testament calls her "the queen of Sheba," and the historian who first set down her story would know exactly where and what Sheba was, and would know that the term would be equally intelligible to all his contemporary readers. Sheba was then as well established, as apparently permanent as Babylon or Egypt. Hundreds of years later Christ, referring to her, called her "the queen of the south": Josephus says that she was queen of Egypt and Ethiopia: his commentator says definitely that she was queen of Sabea in South Arabia.

Where then was Sheba, a country that allowed itself to be ruled by an inquisitive, headstrong woman?

One of the legends comes down in favour of Ethiopia and says that one of the things she took back with her was a son in her womb and that from him and his offspring is derived the Semitic strain still visible in the ruling class of Abyssinia. But the Book of Kings is praiseworthily frank about Solomon and his women; he "loved many strange women, together with the daughter of Pharaoh, women of the Moabites, Ammonites, Edomites, Zidonians and Hittites"; why, if he had loved the queen of Sheba, should the historian have shown this unusual reticence?

Of Egypt she was not queen. Solomon had married Pharaoh's daughter. Nor was Egypt then regarded as "the utmost parts of the earth."

Whether then she ruled in Ethiopia or in Arabia is not of importance. Sheba has gone, its name by virtue of this one story has outlived its geographical identification. The story matters; not because of the legends that have mossed themselves over it, nor because "the half was not told me" and "there was no more spirit in her" have become phrases current amongst many who could not tell their origin, but because, in her own way, this queen of the south is an example of a certain type of female psychology.

She was a woman who was performing satisfactorily what was considered to be a man's job. Queens in their own right were rare in that day, and who knows what intrigues, what prejudices this woman had met and overcome in order to be, and to remain, "queen of the south"? The material success had spelled disaster for the female in her; Elizabeth Tudor is a parallel case. Driving force and enterprise and combativeness are not natural feminine traits, and the women in whom they are born or engendered by circumstance are never wholly happy or at one with their world.

This queen of Sheba's approach to Solomon was antagonistic. In her own country she had heard of his glory; to his great inheritance he had added the final subjection of the Canaanite tribes; he had allied himself by marriage to the ruling house of Egypt; he had built—with the help of Phoenician labour and material such a Temple and such a palace as had never been seen before. And he was wise; even in his own day his knowledge of philosophy and of what we now call psychology was legendary. His existence and his reputation were a challenge to this queen in her own right. She could not—because she did not wish to—believe the reports she had heard about him. Secretly she thought that having made, or maintained, herself queen of Sheba she was the shrewdest and most glorious monarch in the world. Nor were her claims empty; Josephus says "she was inquisitive into philosophy and one that on other accounts also was to be admired."

She could not resist the challenge of Solomon; so she came from her far country "to prove him with hard questions." And she arrived in Jerusalem with "a very great train, with camels that bare spices and very much gold and precious stones." Woman militant, possessive, exhibitionist. Competition between kings can be extravagant enough as the Field of the Cloth of Gold, that meeting between Henry VIII and Francis of France, proves, but when a subtle sexual element is added extravagance knows no bounds. One can imagine her, half confident, half diffident, rigging out her attendants so that her lowest menial, she hopes, will exceed Solomon in all his glory; she hopes, she almost believes. And all the gold and all the spices and all the precious stones, they are to be given to this great king of Israel, not out of generosity alone, but out of an oblique egoism.

Her impressive train and the gifts that were in it are described, but of the "hard questions" the Old Testament tells us nothing. Did she dress eight children, four boys and four girls in identical clothes and demand that Solomon detect their sex? And did he call for bowls of water and say, "Wash your hands," and did they thus betray themselves? Who shall say?

And did Solomon, crafty in his turn, order that between the throne and the entry to the throne-room a stream of water should flow so that the queen of Sheba, approaching him, must perforce lift her skirts and show whether the rumor of a deformed foot were true or not? No one can say that either. But it is interesting to note that about these queens in their own right this hint of a physical deformity hangs. Elizabeth Tudor again, "her mind is as crooked as her carcase," someone said. Was it Sheba's deformed foot, with its implied bar to ordinary sexual attractiveness and achievement that had turned her towards an interest in philosophy? Another unanswerable question.

We only know that Solomon received her graciously and answered all her questions. For at Gibeon, before ever the Temple was planned or the palace, before even Solomon had become settled on the throne, God had appeared to him in a dream and asked him what he most wished for and Solomon had chosen wisdom, "an understanding heart." And there can be no doubt that he understood, not merely the questions which this woman set him, but the motives and farreaching reasons for her visit. He probably both respected and pitied her, for that is the male attitude towards women of her kind. He respected her rank and her wealth and her intelligence, and he pitied her because he had no desire to add her to the seven hundred women, wives and concubines who ministered to his pleasure. And she, who had intended to impress him with her entourage and her wit, was completely deflated. "There was no more spirit in her"; and the completeness of that deflation betrays, albeit unconsciously, the scope and malice of her original intention. Had she come from curiosity that would have been appeased; from admiration, that would have been increased; from friendliness, that would have been cemented. But she had come out of the intellectual pride and vainglory to which unfeminine women are prone, and gently, without effort or ostentation, Solomon had reduced her.

Yet in the end she is an admirable, not pitiable figure. She is saved by her own integrity. Very frankly she told him that she had not believed the reports which she heard, "I believed not the words, until I came and mine eyes have seen it, and behold, the half was not told me. . . . Happy are thy men, happy are thy servants which stand continually before thee and that hear thy wisdom. . . ." A sweeping, generous, most unfeminine speech. In itself it denies the legend that this woman ever bore Solomon's son, for the child of Sheba and Solomon would have left his mark on history and not depended upon the shape of the Abyssinian nose for a memorial to his existence.

Having made her speech, she presented Solomon with the gifts which she had brought in her train; gifts which had seemed so overwhelmingly splendid when they were loaded upon the camels outside the forgotten palace in her nameless, unidentifiable capital, and which now seemed meagre and poor when offered to this great king in whose realm silver was nothing thought of, and whose drinking vessels were all of gold, and whose navy at Tharshish returned every three years from fantastic, fabulous voyages to far places, bringing "gold and silver, ivory, apes and peacocks." Solomon accepted her presents courteously and in return gave her gifts, "whatsoever she asked," which probably means anything she had chanced to admire, a custom which holds in some Eastern places until this day.

And so she turned and went back to her own country, one of the first women on record to have pitted her wits and her wealth against that of a man in a similar position; one of the first women to learn that there is only one way in which—circumstances being roughly even—women can subjugate men, and that not by wit or wealth.

The humiliation would pass, of course. To the end of her reign, to the end of her days (and we hope that such ends were coincidental) she would remember that she had visited Solomon the Great, and the glamour of her visit would hang about her. And before she reached the end of her journey to her own country there is little doubt that some of her forceful, intrepid spirit would have come back to her and she would be able to think of one question which Solomon had not answered completely, or of one question which, had she thought of it in time, might have defeated him entirely.

Solomon, busy with his women and his kingdom and his

poetry would remember her seldom, and then only as the woman who gave him a greater store of spices than any subsequently seen in Israel, and—they say—the balm or balsam tree which her visit introduced into his kingdom, for women who are "inquisitive into philosophy" seldom mark the hearts of the men they encounter. Yet, of the seven hundred wives and princesses and the three hundred concubines that graced the great king's harem, what trace remains? Whereas Sheba, in its day a rich and powerful country, though lost beyond imaginative recall, has, in the story of its queen and her journey, an undying memorial.

Chapter 16

JEZEBEL

AUTHORIZED VERSION: I *Kings 16:31*—II *Kings 11:37*

"Are we to blame if in Calypso's isle
our very virtues are to magic bent?
or if the first long visions that beguile
the heart of youth become our punishment?
We are the same
Though thus transformed by devils. Are we to blame?"
(*Humbert Wolfe*: REQUIEM)

Too long, too crowded, too bizarre is the thought sequence that takes its origin in this woman's name.

Through the smoke of a thousand blood-stained altars, we see, first a young face, turned inland with the same predatory, onward-pressing stare as looked out over the prows of the galleys that reached Cornwall and forced their way around Africa. Then the clouds of incense part and there are the dogs licking the blood of Naboth. The groves leading up to the high places renew their green, while the prophets of Jehovah fall to the sword until only Elijah is left and he cries that he, too, is bound for destruction. And then the chariots of Jehu thunder past the walls of Jezreel and an old woman leans from a window with a taunt upon her painted lips.

All that in the name, Jezebel.

She is one of the earliest figures in a long and tragic line of princesses who marry the kings of other countries and fail to adapt themselves, or refuse to adapt themselves, and so carry to the end, like a banner, or a perfume, the inescapable taint of their alien blood. There was Henrietta Maria, whom the seventeenth-century Puritans hated and called "the Frenchwoman" until she fled; there was Marie Antoinette who was "the Austrian" until her head rolled into the basket of sawdust under the guillotine; there was Eugénie who was always "the Spaniard" until she was dethroned; and there was Victoria's liberal-minded, well-meaning daughter, the ninety-day Empress of Germany, who, because she chose an English doctor to attend her husband in his fatal illness, was held responsible for his death. And they are but a few of the women, who, because they are royal and sought in marriage by princes and kings, lose, in the struggle to retain their own nationality, all hope of happiness and of good reputation.

Of these Jezebel was one. She was the daughter of Ethbaal, the king of Tyre, who ruled the small, but immensely wealthy and influential kingdom of Phoenicia on the seaboard of the Mediterranean to the north of Palestine. She married Ahab, king of Israel, and so became one of those princesses, moved about like pawns upon the board of power politics. For the match with Ahab was not, superficially, a good one or worthy of a Phoenician princess. Israel was still an upstart in the eyes of the older nations, and although David and Solomon had spread its boundaries, consolidated its constitution and increased its wealth, it had recently suffered from internal dissolution. Judah had broken away from Israel and both kingdoms were reduced.

Jezebel knew, when the match was made, that she would never rule in the great palace which Solomon had built out of Phoenician materials with the help of Phoenician labour. Palaces even rawer and newer awaited her in Jezreel and Samaria. She was leaving one of the oldest civilisations in the world to become queen of a country only just established after internal strife, a country unused to the rule of kings, a country in which flourished, with intermittent set-backs, a new and inimical cult—the worship of Jehovah. She was bound to despise Israel and everything Israelitish from the very start.

Yet the match was an expedient one. At the moment when Jezebel turned her back on the sea which had cradled her race, and went inland in the wake of the gold and silversmiths, the artificers in ivory and marble, whom the barbarian Jews at the peak of their power had been obliged to borrow from her father's predecessor, Hiram of Tyre, in order to turn their fortified villages into cities and their houses of cedar into palaces and their humble meeting places into temples, there were other things than the comparative status of Phoenicia and Israel to be considered when a marriage contract was made. For all the countries between the Mediterranean and the inland desert had come under the threat of the growing power and the increasing aggressiveness of Assyria, and they knew that allegiance was vital to survival. Ahab of Israel had already proved himself to be an able soldier; his name, and the forces which he could command, figured large in the list of allies who had combined to oppose the southward sweep of the Assyrian Empire. And marriage was still one of the best ways of cementing an alliance. So Jezebel, princess of Tyre, if she had entertained higher hopes, more soaring ambitions, must forget them and go to seal the alliance between Phoenicia and Israel. It was very unfortunate for her; unfortunate, at times, for Israel, but Israel survived and Jezebel has gone down to history as a painted, evil woman.

Of her physical appearance we are told nothing. The chroniclers of Israel were well capable, upon occasion, of awarding, in a few words, the accolade of beauty; about Jezebel they are silent. Nor would they have done her justice, for Ahab's marriage to her was unpopular from the very beginning. The historians were ignorant of—or chose to be blind to—the reason for this alliance between Phoenicia and Israel and from the very first attributed it to Ahab's wickedness. Their attitude towards Jezebel is set down in a single, very revealing sentence:— "And it came to pass, as if it had been a light thing for him (that is Ahab) to walk in the sins of Jeroboam . . . that he took to wife Jezebel, the daughter of Ethbaal, king of the Zidonians."

But that sentence reveals more than the writer's prejudice. It says plainly that Ahab had already followed in the steps of Jeroboam who had set up the bull images in Israel and ordered the people to worship them. Ahab was an idolater before he married Jezebel. And she, of course, had been reared to the worship of Baal.

Despite the silence upon the subject it is possible that she was beautiful. It is, at least, very easy to imagine her olive-skinned, lustrous-eyed and of proud demeanour. Tawny hair, for some reason, suggests itself—as it does in the case of Mary Magdalene —but the thought has no reference to fact, it is the irresponsible association of ideas. That her looks may not have been Semitic is more than likely. Some authorities hold that the Phoenicians originated in Crete, and their love of their sea, and their mastership of it—not Semitic traits—supports if it does not prove the theory.

It is even possible that her difference in appearance from the Jewish women would account for her unpopularity with her subjects and for Ahab's infatuation for her. Foreign wives, though viewed with prejudice and hatred by the masses, do tend to exercise great influence over the men they marry, and "whoring after strange women" is not just a Biblical figure of speech. That Ahab loved and trusted and respected her is made plain at each turn of her story and it is noticeable that although he was a young man when he married her, and although tradition entitled him to a full harem, no other woman even attains the importance of being named, either as secondary wife, or concubine, during the years of his reign.

Whether she brought beauty to the raw barbaric court of Ahab we cannot know. The story concerns itself with what she did bring beyond all doubt—the cult of Baal. Baal worship was as natural to her as breathing. The Phoenicians worshipped two gods, Baal and Astoreth, male and female. Ethbaal, before he became king of the country, had been a priest in the service of Astoreth, and Jezebel, before her marriage had been a priestess of Baal. Her adherence to the faith of her fathers, her fanatic passion for the religion in which she had been reared, must be judged as loyalty or bigotry according to the bigotry or the tolerance of the assessor.

But the point was that the Jews could not afford to be tolerant. Tolerance is for the sure, the established. And the worshippers of

Jehovah were slowly, painfully sloughing off their belief in the old gods of Canaan and reaching out for a new, purer, more spiritual conception of godhead. Baal, upon whom they had turned their backs, was the god of nature, of the hills and the groves and the streams; he could be symbolised by material things; he could be placated by gifts, flattered, bribed and exhorted. Jehovah, the Absolute, towards whom they were groping, was a spirit to be touched, enshrined and worshipped only by the spirit and mind of man. So Baal and Jehovah must be forever in opposition.

Jezebel, who was, after all, a "religious" woman, probably spent some time during her early days in Israel in a careful, sceptical study of Jehovah worship. And if she did so she would have observed that the Jews, grappling with this new and revolutionary idea of God, had not yet succeeded in evolving a new *form* of worship. In many ways the rites and ceremonies were indistinguishable. Even the idea of human sacrifice had only recently been abandoned; Abraham had attempted to sacrifice Isaac; Jephthah had succeeded in sacrificing his daughter. The stream of bullocks and lambs and doves which went up to Jehovah's altar—and which were to continue to do so until Christ's own day—were in no way different from those which went up to the high places of Baal; the methods of sacrifice (as we learn from the story of Elijah and the Baalites on Carmel) were perilously akin. It was extremely easy for the ordinary, not-specially-inspired bulk of the people of Israel to become confused, to worship now Jehovah, now Baal and sometimes both.

So to Jezebel, when she came from a country where Baal's supremacy had never been challenged, it would seem a very easy thing to reclaim the erring country of Israel for Baal. In a somewhat similar spirit Mary Tudor, centuries later, mounted the throne of England and kindled the fires of Smithfield.

That she intended to adhere to her own religion and, if possible, to reclaim Israel, is made clear by the fact she brought her priests with her. They were to be the nucleus of the great body of Baalites which she meant to assemble. They rode in her train with a number of Phoenician ladies, chosen, some for their skill in various arts, some for their social qualities, for the Phoenician princess was going to live in a barbarian country and must take her court with her. And behind them came the baggage train, camels and asses well-burdened with robes and jewels and carpets and hangings and ornaments for the beautifying of the raw new palace, with presents from Ethbaal to his son-in-law, and with the bowls and knives and candlesticks and censors of the priests' craft. The watchmen on the tower of Jezreel saw the cloud of dust which announced the caravan's approach, and Ahab, warned in time, rode out to meet his bride.

Theirs is not, upon the surface, a love story. Never, even during its most intimate phases, is there a word or an inflexion of tenderness. But of course the whole story is overcharged with the noise of religions and nations at war with one another; the softer, the lute music of love might well be drowned. But something gave Jezebel a tremendous ascendancy over Ahab; he confided in her; he accepted her judgement; he never made the slightest attempt either to control her or rebuke her. One is left with the impression that Ahab, king of Israel and brave soldier as he was, lacked the strength of character and the ruthlessness that might have made this fiery princess respect him. And with such women there can be no lasting love without respect, without even an element of fear. It is a pity; for some overmastering emotional attachment might have weaned her from Baal; and a stronger man, a loved man, might have persuaded her to restraint over the matter of religion if only for the sake of her own popularity. As it is, her story is full of the sound and fury of religious strife, and Jezebel, who had the courage and the vigour and the resourcefulness which would have made her a good queen for a young struggling country, has left behind her only the memory of brutal persecution in the interests of a creed already outworn and almost rejected, the sad haunting story of Naboth and his vineyard and the deathless, if misleading epithet "a painted Jezebel."

Upon her arrival in Israel she lost no time in establishing her priests and letting it be known that in future the god of the Zidonians would be the god of Israel. In another manner and in another voice she asked Elijah's own question, "How long halt ye between two opinions?" For so far had the Jews gone backward that the greater proportion of them had already, at some time or another "bowed the knee" to Baal; and from the people themselves she appears to have met with little opposition. Nor from Ahab, already tainted, and in any case not equipped to oppose the will of his tumultuous, bigoted young bride.

But there was, nevertheless, some opposition. There were some priests of Jehovah who were prepared to be martyred rather than turn to Baal; and there was Elijah the prophet, the man of the desert, "hairy and girt with a leather girdle"; and there was, perhaps most interesting because most secret, an enemy whom Jezebel never suspected, an enemy who never declared himself, Obadiah, steward of Ahab's household, an intimate, a confidant of the king.

It was not in Jezebel's royal, violent and unreasonable nature to brook opposition from anyone; so the priests of Jehovah were put to the sword, Elijah fled before her threats, and it was left to the smooth, unsuspected Obadiah to hide a hundred of the doomed prophets by fifties in a cave and to smuggle to them enough bread and water to maintain them alive. Obadiah deserves a moment's regard, even though the story be Jezebel's. He was, like another famous character, "a fearful man"; his character is limned in the few telling lines that are characteristic of Bible history. Obadiah "feared the Lord greatly," but that fear did not, as it did with some men, drive out all other trepidations. He feared to give offence; he feared to lose his life; and it is implicit in the story that he feared to lose his position. But he is a symbol of the silent, stubborn thing which survives the blizzard of persecution. Given a greater courage, a tendency to heroism and he too would have been slain by Jezebel, together with the last hundred of the prophets.

So far as eye could see Israel had reverted to Baal; the nucleus of Baal's priesthood had been reinforced, Samaria the new capital boasted a temple to Baal, the groves which led up to the outdoor altars were flourishing. Jezebel could be satisfied.

But Elijah still lived, and it was he who sent a message to Ahab saying that there was to be a great drought, followed by a great famine in the land. Control of the weather is always considered a divine prerogative by primitive peoples, and by many not so primitive—a prolonged drought will, even nowadays, evoke a "Prayer for Rain" in some English churches. And in this particular respect Jehovah had pre-empted the powers of the old nature gods who had been deposed; a drought was a sign of His displeasure, the rain a proof of forgiveness. This drought was considered by Elijah, and by all the faithful in Israel, to be the result of the reversal to Baal worship. Elijah made his threat and then retired, first to the brook Cherith and then to the house of the widow of Zarepath, who was a fellow-countrywoman of Jezebel, for Zarepath lay about midway between Tyre and Zidon.

The drought and the famine are historical facts. They are mentioned by writers who were impartial to this war between Jezebel and Elijah, Baal and Jehovah. It was not confined to the borders of Israel; Ethbaal, Jezebel's father, suffered from it as severely as Ahab. And when it reached its height, when panic and fear had seized all Israel even Ahab, the king, Elijah came back, defying Jezebel, and staged upon Mount Carmel such a drama as has never been equalled either in historic fact or literary invention.

So far as one can read this was one time when Ahab did not consult Jezebel. Through the agency of Obadiah Ahab met Elijah who ordered him to call all Israel to Mount Carmel and to send thither also the eight hundred and fifty priests of Baal. Ahab obeyed him implicitly, and Jezebel is nowhere mentioned in this part of the narrative.

So, empty-bellied, drawn of face, utterly beaten of spirit, the Israelites came to Carmel, wondering what they were to see, or to hear, not knowing then what excitement awaited them. There were the two altars, one tended by the priests of Baal, four hundred of whom were accustomed to eat at Jezebel's table, and who were doubtless the last of all to feel the pinch of famine; the other tended by a solitary, hairy, leather-girt man whose apparent confidence and defiance were very near despair, and who, before many hours had passed, was to be beseeching God to take away his life. And there were the two lean, famine-wrecked bullocks, similarly slain and hewn into bleeding lumps. And then there was the demand to the unseen powers. For, as Elijah argued with bitter logic, either Baal was God, or Jehovah was, and it was time the matter was settled. Let the one who sent down fire from heaven to light his own altar and consume his sacrifice be God from henceforth.

At this point we come nearer than at any other time to seeing the priests of Baal in action. Elijah gave them the advantage of making the first test. And there in its full flowering, before the eyes of all Israel was the thing which Jezebel had passionately sponsored and Ahab encouraged—the ritual of Baal, with its frenzied dancing, and its frenzied shouting and its frenzied self-mutilation. For hours of the burning hot day it lasted, while Elijah mocked, saying, of Baal, "either he is talking, or he is pursuing, or he is on a journey, or peradventure he sleepeth and must be awakened." But there was "no voice, nor any that answered." And noonday passed and the afternoon wore away.

There were, we must think, honest Baal worshippers amongst them; men who believed, as Jezebel believed, that it was well within Baal's power to send down fire from heaven, and that the failure was within themselves. They, more than the others, would become mad, ready to indulge in the wildest frenzy if only it could attract the god's attention. And then there were the others, the time-servers, the self-seekers, who, as the hours wore on and the sacrifice began to reek in the sun, would think mainly of what Jezebel the Queen would have to say about their failure. And all the time Elijah's stare grew more sardonic and triumphant, his taunts more barbed, while on the slopes below the altars the mass of the people waited, thinking of their ruined crops, their starved beasts, their hungry children and their empty bellies, and watched for a sign, any sign.

And then it was evening, and the unsurpassable moment came. Elijah ceased his taunting and put on dignity like a garment. Calling for the people to come near him, he ordered his altar to be drenched with water. Three times the barrels of precious, hard come-by liquid splashed out before the eyes of the thirst-tormented crowd, until the wood and the stones and the meat were soaked and the surplus stood in the trench that he had made around the altar. Elijah by this time had the measure of his adversary, and knew that he must allow no possibility of any suggestion of sleight-of-hand or chicanery to exist.

He did not dance, or slash his flesh with a knife; he spoke clearly, with dignified humility to his God, addressing him in terms which struck home to every Jewish heart, loyal or wavering in that vast assembly. . . . "Lord God of Abraham, Isaac and of Israel. . . ." (And that one does not need to have Jewish blood to respond to that sequence of words the maker of the film "Proud Valley" proved.) "Let it be known this day that thou art God in Israel."

And it was known; for we read that the fire fell and consumed the burnt sacrifice and the wood and the stones and the dust, even the water that was in the trench it licked up. And the people fell on their faces and cried, "The Lord He is the God; the Lord He is the God." Then at Elijah's command they fell upon the prophets of Baal and not one of them escaped.

That night the drought broke. At first, in the sky which had for so long known no cloud, a little cloud, "like a man's hand," and then "the heaven was dark with clouds and wind and there was a great rain."

Ahab, with his weathercock heart veering towards Jehovah and Elijah, was faced with the duty of telling Jezebel all he had seen and heard that day. Did he hope that she would be persuaded, and so persuade him? Vain hope. The only thing in the whole story that had any significance for her was the fact that Elijah had dared to slay her prophets. He had forecast the drought, he had brought down fire from heaven and he had foretold the coming of the saving rain, but none of that mattered at all. He had slain the prophets of Baal. So she sent him a message, "So let the gods do to me, and more also, if I make not thy life as the life of one of these by tomorrow about this time." It would take her at least until tomorrow to find a man of her own mind, capable of performing the deed. But it is, in a way, a tribute to Jezebel that Elijah, despite his recent triumph, his faith in his God, and the feeling which he must have experienced—that all Israel was on his side—fled away into the neighbouring kingdom of Judah, where, in due time he received orders to go and anoint Hazael of Damascus to be king of Syria (he was to bring death to Ahab), Jehu to be king of Israel (he was to bring death to Ahab's son), and to select Elisha as his own successor.

Of all this Jezebel knew nothing; back in the cities of Samaria and Jezreel she was busily and determinedly restoring the religion in which she believed. Had she acted like Obadiah and hidden some of her prophets, or did riders on swift camels go hastening into Tyre for fresh recruits? And if so, what enthusiasm, what missionary zeal must have been needed to take any priest of Baal into Israel where even the queen had not been able to prevent the slaughter of Carmel!

But in her rather uphill task of recapturing Israel a second time for Baal, Jezebel paused for a moment to give Ahab a lesson in kingship and the Jews a lesson in behavior.

There was, in Jezreel, a man called Naboth who had inherited from his father a vineyard which adjoined the king's palace. The vineyard was older than the palace which had been erected by Ahab's father, for Naboth speaks of the vineyard as being the inheritance of his fathers. There they were, next door to one another, the new palace and the old vineyard, and one day, Ahab, looking out from the palace windows, conceived the idea of buying the vineyard and turning it into a garden of herbs whose fragrance, drawn out by the sun, would rise and permeate the courts and corridors of the palace. Probably it was at first an idle notion, which grew until it became a desire and then—for there was a good deal of the spoilt child in Ahab—an urgent necessity.

Despite the evil things that he did and allowed to be done, there was something not entirely unlikable about Ahab. He set about this business in a typically blunt and honest manner. As a Jew he had a respect for property, especially for inherited property, so he sent for Naboth and put the suggestion to him as though there were no difference between their ranks. He would, he said, buy the vineyard for its proper worth in money, or he would give him a better vineyard. But Naboth was also a Jew, with a respect for property, especially inherited property, and he made it perfectly clear in that first interview that he intended to pass on to his son, exact and intact, the property that he had inherited from his father. And Ahab, a Jew, accepted the refusal; he neither argued nor threatened; he knew that ancestors were more important than kings, and he knew that never, never, would he have that herb garden. He was bitterly disappointed, sulky, almost heart-broken, but left to himself he would never have lifted a finger to harm Naboth who was, as he knew, well within his rights.

But with Jezebel it was very different. She saw Ahab sulking about the palace, and soon discovered the reason for his mood, and to her, the princess from Tyre, it seemed that Naboth's behaviour was both ungracious and wicked. Jezebel had been reared in the tradition of what another royal line, centuries later, was to call the Divine Right of Kings. In her time it was so implicitly understood that except to a barbarian race like the Jews it needed no explanation at all. In every other country the idea of royalty was inextricably mingled with the idea of divinity. In every other country to have refused the king anything he desired would have been as bad as refusing a sacrifice to the reigning god. In no other country would that vineyard have been allowed to jostle the palace; in no other country would such an offer have been made between king and commoner. Jezebel had now lived in Israel for some years, and she knew, in her mind, the attitude of the people towards their king, but she still did not understand it, still resented it, was still infuriated by it, and now, since it had come between Ahab and something he desired, she determined to strike at it.

It reads as though she were fond of him as a mother is fond of a child. When he told her about his disappointment there was no tenderness, no sympathy in her manner, it was bracing almost to the point of being scornful. "Dost thou now govern the kingdom of Israel?" she asked. Are you a king or are you not?

In actual words she said to him, "Arise and eat bread and let thine heart be merry: *I* will give thee the vineyard of Naboth the Jezreelite." Ahab, who had, by his mood, admitted the thing to be impossible, did not say "How?" or ask what means Jezebel intended to adopt. There is the measure, both of his trust in her, and of his guilt. Naboth's death should rest more heavily upon Ahab than upon Jezebel; for the king, a Jew, recognised Naboth's right; to Jezebel such right had no existence at all; and when she set men, wicked men, hired men, sons of Belial, up on high to say that Naboth had blasphemed God and the king, *she* at least believed in the validity of the charge. Naboth had refused the king something, and since royalty and divinity were linked, therefore he had blasphemed.

So Naboth, a victim in the conflict between national traditions, went down to a horrible death beneath the stones, and Jezebel, as soon as she knew that he was dead, hurried away to tell Ahab that the vineyard was his and that he could proceed with his plans for making the herb garden. Ahab again asked no question. Immured in his palace, isolated in his mood, had he heard no whispers, been deaf to the pack-cry of the stone-throwers? Even so, he must have heard the triumphant gloating in Jezebel's voice as she said, "Arise, take possession of the vineyard of Naboth the Jezreelite, which he refused to give thee for money." And the death of Naboth must have seemed unnaturally opportune. But Ahab accepted the information, and the vineyard, as unquestioningly as a child accepts a present from its mother; and went down immediately to order the uprooting of the mature, full-bearing vines and plan the herb garden for which he hankered.

And it was there that Elijah found him; and there, between the doomed vines, the prophet of the desert spoke the doom of Ahab and of all his house. And behind those words Ahab recognised the authority which had ordered the drought and the famine, commanded the obedient fire on Carmel and released the rain over Israel. Ahab must have left the vineyard on that evening more miserable than on the former occasion. For Elijah had said that in the very place where the dogs had licked the innocent blood of Naboth, there they should lick Ahab's; and Jezebel, dominant, intrepid, crafty Jezebel, the dogs should have her too, not her blood only, but her very flesh and bones, under the wall of the city which she now ruled.

Did she meet him this time and wonder, and ask, what ailed him? If not she would know on the morrow: for Ahab had no resources in himself; he would turn to her for comfort in the big matter as in the small; and there can be no doubt as to her method for restoring his confidence and making his heart merry again. Despite all the recent happenings her belief in Baal was unshaken; Jehovah might threaten, Jehovah's prophet foretell evil things, she—and Ahab with her—could ignore it all, resting their faith in Baal.

For outwardly nothing changed. In the vineyard Ahab might tear his clothes and humble himself, but he was incapable of doing the one thing which might have averted his doom—going into the palace and telling Jezebel that her rule was over and that Baal's temple and grove and priesthood were no longer acceptable in Israel.

So the story moved on to its inexorable end.

Ahab went to war against Syria, against the king of Syria who had been specially appointed to be his undoing. The king of Israel died bravely. Wounded in the chest by a "bow drawn at a venture," he remained "stayed up" in his chariot until evening, lest the news of his hurt should discourage his forces and sway the tide of the battle. But at nightfall he died, having lived long enough to know that Israel had been defeated; and they took his body to Samaria and buried him there. But the prophecy of Elijah had been fulfilled nonetheless, for the chariot, spattered with Ahab's life blood, went down to the pool for cleansing, and there the dogs licked it.

Jezebel lived for fourteen years more. For two of them she stood behind the throne of her son Ahaziah (whom Ahab in one of his wavering moments had named "Jehovah Holds"), and for twelve more she ruled through another son, Jehoram, still forcing her religion upon the country of her adoption, defying Elisha as she had defied Elijah. And then the time was ripe for the rest of the words spoken in that evening vineyard to be fulfilled; the moment came for Jezebel to sit down to her mirror and perform a gallant gesture which was to make her name an epithet, a dart still sharp upon the tongue of the spiteful after all these centuries of years.

When she sat down to paint her face, her room in the palace of Jezreel was the only room in the city which panic had not already invaded; hers was, perhaps, the only hand steady enough to apply the paint with skill. For there had been a new revolution in Israel, and Jehu, a common soldier whom Elijah had anointed secretly after the drama of Carmel, had been anointed by Elisha, and had announced his kingship. Jehoram and all the rest of Ahab's house had been wiped out, and all the priests of Baal, gathered by Jehu's guile into one place, had been put to the sword. The city of Jezreel, conscious of having been the city of Ahab, of Jezebel and of Baal, now waited with bated breath the coming of the avenger. Many people had already hurried out to meet Jehu and to make their peace with him. In the half-deserted palace in a half-deserted city, Jezebel, with her attendant eunuchs for company, sat down to lay upon cheek and lip the colour and bloom of youth.

When she was painted and dressed and ornamented to her liking, she moved to the window and stood looking out over the city to which she had come as a young bride, the city in which she had wielded such enormous influence. The high wall, gilded at the top by the sunshine, ran steeply down into the indigo shadow at its foot, and in the shadow lurked the slinking shapes of the lean-ribbed pariah dogs, the eaters of refuse, the scavengers of every Eastern city. Their like had licked the blood of Ahab, and now these were waiting. Jehu was coming; war was in the air; the dogs would feed full before morning.

What could her thoughts have been? We have no clue, save in the negation of clue. She was not penitent; of that we must be certain. One word, one hint from her at that moment, that her long enmity to Jehovah, her long loyalty to Baal, had been mistaken, would have been seized upon, how avidly, by the historian. Twice she had built up her priesthood, twice had it been destroyed; every word that Jehovah had uttered through Elijah or Elisha had been fulfilled, or seemed likely to be fulfilled. She was alone now with her unavailing, discredited god.

But there is no sign of weakening in this old woman. She was not convinced; nor was she frightened—her greeting of Jehu proves that. Nor was she, as has so often been suggested, prepared to play the harlot with Jehu in order to preserve her life. That error arises from the working method of the prostitutes of the East who put on their finery and pose at the open windows of the streets where they ply their trade. To paint the face and to look from a window may have been a harlot's action, but Jezebel was no harlot. Even the prejudiced historian, "extreme to mark what was done amiss," never lays that to her charge. For although, in the past she must have been guilty of some of the sexual excesses that were part of the very fabric of Baal's ritual, she was now too old, too proud, too defiant to offer herself to Jehu. Besides she was not a fool, and only a fool could have thought that Jehovah's specifically self-appointed instrument could be seduced by the painted face of a woman grown old in Baal's service.

And what of her greeting to the conquering usurper? When the chariots of Jehu—that furious driver, thundered under the wall, and the checked horses pawed in the dust, Jezebel leaned from her window and cried, "Had Zimri peace who slew *his* master?" And the words would fall, as she knew they would fall, cold and ominous upon the ear of a man flushed with victory. For Zimri too had been a soldier, a leader of the chariots; Zimri too had slain his king and completely exterminated the royal house. And Zimri's reign had lasted for exactly seven days. "Had Zimri peace who slew his master?" Nothing the woman could have said could have been more pertinent, more mocking, more disturbing. But because of the paint on her face, the superb courage, the truly royal pride of Jezebel's approach to the conqueror had been obscured until this moment.

Jehu was so much stung by her question that he issued an order which he afterwards regretted, because it was not for him, anointed into royalty, to bring so ignominious an end upon one of royal blood. But the order was not his, in actual truth, either to issue or to withhold. The words had been spoken years before, in the green quiet spaces between the trussed vines that a man named Naboth had tended.

So Jehu, taunted and angry, looked up and said, "Who is on my side? Who?" And two or three eunuchs looked out of the window. Then he said what it was ordained that he should say, "Throw her down." And the eunuchs, perhaps very willingly, since Jezebel can hardly have been an easy or indulgent mistress, threw her down. The hooves of the horses, the wheels of the chariot crushed out the life of the most-feared, most-hated, most powerful queen that Israel ever knew. When the chariots moved on, the dogs surged forward in the sudden quiet and began their undiscriminating orgy. So the words of the prophecy were fulfilled. Under the walls of Jezreel, the dogs ate Jezebel.

Later, over his supper, Jehu ordered that she should be given a decent burial because "she is a king's daughter." (And he was now a king; he would have daughters of his own). He also called her "a cursed woman" thereby showing far more perspicacity than he realised. For she was a cursed woman. Born and reared in one faith, loyal to it, active in its interests, never once meeting, not in Ahab, not in Elijah, not Elisha, a personality capable of influencing her own, deaf to persuasion, impervious to logic, what is that but to be a cursed woman? Born untimely? Predestined to be an evil mommet in the great drama of history? A bad stubborn woman? Does it matter now? She painted her face and went to her death bravely. How can anyone who has not yet faced that tremendous experience assess her final worth?

Chapter 17

NAAMAN'S WIFE'S LITTLE MAID

AUTHORIZED VERSION: II *Kings 5*

"True wisdom join'd with simpleness."
(*Henry Howard, Earl of Surrey*: MEANS TO ATTAIN A HAPPY LIFE)

A story which begins with the dragging away of a young girl into slavery and ends with the transmission of a deadly disease, hardly seems to qualify for the description "a pleasant story." Yet the story of the little Jewess who became bondmaid to the wife of the captain of the hosts of Syria is actually one of the most nearly "pretty" stories of all the stories in the Bible which concern women. And since its pleasantness rests almost entirely in the character of the little girl herself, she deserves a place in this chronicle, though the mention of her in the Old Testament is very brief and uninformative.

The thing happened during the lifetime of the prophet Elisha. Israel, led by an idolatrous king, had been guilty of backsliding and as a punishment had been defeated by the Syrians who were led by Naaman. One company of Syrians had taken some captives and amongst them was this little nameless girl whom Naaman presented to his wife. The child thus became both an exile and a slave.

It is impossible for the twentieth century eye to regard the words "slave" or "slavery" with any kind of equanimity, for our view is all coloured by the exposures and revelations made during the eighteenth and early nineteenth centuries when people were working for the abolition of slavery in the Southern States of America. For anyone who has read these "atrocity" stories of another generation, even that comely ornament known as a "slave bracelet" can call up horrid visions of cane-fields in Louisiana, cotton fields in Georgia, sugar mills in the Barbados. But in the ancient world to be a slave did not necessarily imply that one lived in a state of unmitigated, abject misery. Many a slave in an Eastern household lived a life preferable to that of any technically "free" man at any time say, between the fall of Rome and the thirties of the nineteenth century. For one thing, in those days of greater leisure, of slower living pace, a slave with any ability or personality was bound to be noticed, promoted, favoured, and very probably in time given his freedom. And in those pastoral, patriarchal times there was no temptation to exploit slave labour for monetary gain. The owning of slaves, was, with a few exceptions, a custom, part of a way of life, rather than a business. (From this statement one exempts the dye industry of Tyre. "Purple stuff from Tyre" was dearly come by.)

It may be likely that this little Jewess found life in Naaman's household preferable to that in her own home. If she came from a family where there were brothers and brothers-in-law, and a father to be waited upon, from a house where from sun-up to sun-down she was fetching water and cooking meals, and spinning and weaving, and gathering fuel, and mending, and sweeping floors, she probably found her life as a personal maid almost unbelievably pleasant and easy. It all depended upon the temperament of her mistress. And that this was a pleasant one is evidenced by the freedom with which the child could talk to her. Not even the most intimate subject was forbidden.

And there was, in the household of Naaman, one subject at least which must be handled tactfully. For Naaman, this great general, this important and honoured man, was a leper.

Leprosy was, of course, horribly prevalent in the East in that day, and though to us, familiar with the "leper squints" in churches and the story of the bells ringing and the voices crying, "Unclean, unclean," it may seem strange that a man so afflicted should have pursued his career as a soldier and married a woman and in every way gone on with his normal life, it is a fact of all Eastern peoples that the Jews were the only race which had any rules regarding the segregation of lepers. The Book of Leviticus is the origin of that cry, "Unclean, unclean," and though the treatment which it orders is unscientific, all concerned with visits to the priest and the sacrifice of turtle doves and other semi-magical rites, it all goes to prove that the Jews were the first people to suspect, or believe, that lepers should be set apart from those whose flesh was whole and clean.

So at first, perhaps, the little Jewess would be astonished and faintly shocked to see Naaman pursuing his ordinary life. But time went on and she found him a kind master, and she liked her mistress, and obviously she either bore no resentment against her fate, or was a girl of almost unbelievably sweet and forgiving nature; for one day she burst out into quite vehement speech, "Would God," she exclaimed, "my lord were with the prophet that is in Samaria! For he would recover him of his leprosy."

She had grown up, one sees, within the radius of Elisha's fame. What stories she had heard! The children had mocked Elisha because of his bald head, and he had called up bears from the wood to devour them; Elisha had sprinkled some salt into the bitter, undrinkable water at Jericho and it had "been healed," Elisha had promised the childless Sunamite a son, and the child had been born in due time; and then he had died and Elisha had restored him to life. There was no end to the legend of Elisha, there was no limit to Elisha's power. The healing of a leper would be nothing to him!

Was she proud, this little Israelite? Israel had lost a battle and she had lost her freedom, but Israel had one thing which Syria, so wealthy, so successful and pleasant had not, a prophet who could work miracles. Or was she humble? They have been kind to me, the least I can do is to make this suggestion! Or did she speak from a mixture of motives?

The important thing was that they took heed of her. Reared in the Beecher Stowe tradition of slavery, cutting our poetic teeth on "Beside the ungathered rice he lay, his sickle in his hand," it is a little surprising to us that a vehement exclamation wrung out of a slave girl should have gained so much attention. But it did. Before even the wife of Naaman, who would, one feels, have been the person most anxious for his cure, could rise from her dressing table and seek her husband, another attendant had hurried away with the report, "Thus and thus said the maid that is of the land of Israel."

And Naaman despised neither the information nor its source. On the contrary he carried the story to his master, so that the words of the little Jewish slave girl were reported within the walls of the palace of the king of Syria, and the king, whose army had conquered that of the king of Israel, immediately despatched a valuable present and a letter which proved that he had not listened very closely to what he had been told, for the letter demanded that the *king* of Israel, not the prophet of Israel, should cure Naaman of his leprosy.

And the king of Israel was quite distraught. He rent his clothes and cried, "Am I God, to kill and to make alive that this man doth send unto me to recover a man of his leprosy? Wherefore consider I pray you and see how he seeketh a quarrel against me." For Israel was weak in those days, and its king felt that almost any invented excuse would serve to bring the Syrian hordes against him again. But when Elisha heard about the letter and about the king's distress he said, "Let him come now to me and he shall know that there is a prophet in Israel."

So the little bondmaid saw her master set out with his horses and his chariot for the house of the prophet about whom she had told him. And whoever had doubts that day in Syria, she had none. She was certain that when Naaman returned he would be like other men, his leprosy gone. And all because of her!

But when Naaman returned he was still a leper, and he was in a raging bad temper. What had happened, the little maid wondered. Was it that the Israelitish prophet had refused to heal a Syrian? Then she heard the story. Elisha had not refused to cure Naaman, but he had grossly insulted him. He had sent out word that the general had only to bathe himself seven times in the river Jordan and he would be healed. As though an application of water . . . as though Jordan, that miserable little river . . . "Are not Abana and Pharpar, rivers of Damascus, better than all the waters of Israel? May I not wash in them and be clean?" Naaman demanded in a rage, and turned and went away.

It was, the Old Testament says, "his servants" who came and spoke words of reason to him. And in the absence of any specific evidence to the contrary may we not imagine that the little Jewess was one of those servants, perhaps the vocal one? It was, after all, she who had suggested the visit to Elisha, she felt responsible for its outcome, anxious that she, and Elisha and Israel, should be justified. And the words which brought Naaman to his senses have a sweet reasonableness, a gentleness, and withal, a shrewdness in tune with this child's character. "My father, if the prophet had bid thee do some great thing, wouldest thou not have done it? How much rather then when he saith to thee, Wash and be clean?"

So Naaman was persuaded and went and dipped himself in Jordan and the miracle came about.

The story of how he offered Elisha an enormous reward and how Elisha refused it, and how the servant Gehazi ran after the Syrian's chariot and by a lie extracted two talents of silver and two changes of raiment, and so returned to the prophet laden with riches and "white as snow" with leprosy, has really no place here. And the little Jewess is not mentioned again. Perhaps, in gratitude they gave her her freedom and a little money to be her dowry and sent her back to her own people. Or she may have stayed to see a very curious load arrive in Naaman's courtyard—two mules' burden of Israelitish soil, upon which in future Naaman was to perform his secret, his real devotions. For with the healing of his disease the Syrian became a worshipper of Jehovah. Not openly. He took the precaution of telling Elisha that it would still be obligatory for him to accompany his master, the king of Syria, into the house of Rimmon and to go through the gestures of worship there; but they would be but gestures, "Now I know that in all the earth there is no God but in Israel."

So perhaps the little Jewess stayed in Syria and did not return to Israel, instead Israel came to her; and she and her master worshipped Jehovah upon that little mound of sacred soil. In any case her work was done. By some centuries she had forestalled Christ's repudiation of the idea that the Jews had a monopoly of God. She was, in fact, the first missionary; the very first medical missionary.

Chapter 18

ESTHER

AUTHORIZED VERSION: *The Book of Esther*

"He hath put down the mighty from their seats, and exalted them of low degree."

(*The Magnificat*)

It is impossible to read the book of Esther and avoid the thought that here is one of the most perfect historical novels in the world. Few stories are so rich in romance and drama, so full of colour and movement and tension. Against an exotic, voluptuous background the vital and comprehensible characters shape the story; and that story includes love—on the Cophetua and the Beggar Maid theme—intrigue, revenge and hatred, and even holds within its scope a foreshadowing of events which were to stir the history of nations, for in the book of Esther we see the beginning of anti-Semitism, of the ghettos and pogroms of a later day. It is understandable that some commentators look warily upon the story and question its authenticity, for it is so complete and rounded, so entirely satisfactory that it seems to belong to the world of art rather than to that of reality. It is pleasant to think that, despite the recurrent doubts, nothing conclusive has been proved that might banish the book of Esther from the pages of the Bible. And there she stands, the exiled Jewish girl, who became queen of Persia.

When Esther lived the Jews were in captivity. Nebuchadnezzar had finally sacked Jerusalem and carried off the tribes. But his conquest over Palestine had been the last triumph of an already decaying power. After his reign had ended in madness a few troubled kings ruled, each for a brief spell, in Babylon, and then that empire fell, in its turn, under the power of Persia.

The Persian Empire was the furthest flung of any up-to-date, and the king whom Esther was to marry—called Ahasuerus in the Old Testament, and Artaxerxes in other records—claimed to rule "from India even unto Ethiopia." That meant that he controlled—as so many rulers had aspired to do—the great trade routes between the East and the West, and while he could do so his power and his wealth were illimitable.

But those were uncertain days, and it was not until he had been three years upon the throne that Ahasuerus saw fit to celebrate his succession. Then, reasonably safe from usurpers and rivals, he gave two feasts of such Oriental magnificence that their description rivals anything in the Arabian Nights. The first, given to his friends and his Persian officials, lasted for a hundred and eighty days; the second, equally magnificent, since it was designed to impress and delight the ambassadors of other nations who were his sycophants and satellites, was briefer and lasted for seven days.

To house the crowd of guests, he had had built, in the palace grounds of Shushan, another temporary palace, whose pillars were of gold and silver and marble, with hangings of white and blue and green and "purple stuff from Tyre": pavements of marble, red and white, black and blue, were laid upon the floors of it, and the couches upon which the feasters reclined were all of silver and gold. All the drinking vessels were of gold, encrusted with jewels. The loot of a hundred cities was gathered in Shushan then, and the sacred cups from Jehovah's altars as well as those of many a lesser deity were mustered for Ahasuerus' glory. Everything that was most rare and delightful in the way of food and drink, entertainment and decoration, was spread before the king's guests, but when the feast had gone on, with mounting fervour, for seven days, he realised that the most rare and precious thing which he possessed had not been displayed. Vashti, the queen and the most beautiful woman in the world, had, after the manner of Eastern women, remained in her own apartments, where, not to be outdone, she had given lavish entertainments to the women folk of her husband's guests.

Perhaps, after all those days of drinking, manners had grown free and rules had relaxed. Or perhaps in that gathering of mixed nationalities some idle boast had roused a spirit of competition; were Egyptian women lovelier than those of Elam; how did the beauties of Persia compare with those of Phoenicia? For this reason or that, or from no reason save his own inexplicable whim, Ahasuerus felt a desire to display, against all rules, his queen to his guests, so he sent a messenger into the women's palace and asked Vashti to come to the hall of feasting.

She sent him back a blunt refusal, perfectly justified by custom. The king and his guests might have drunk themselves into a state where they could no longer distinguish between what was seemly and what was not, but she was still sensible of her dignity and remembered the rules governing the conduct of women. They did not appear at public feasts.

One can imagine how her women guests would gasp with astonishment at such a request having been made, and at the same time smother their feelings of envy; and how they would giggle together when the chamberlains had hurried back with the queen's message. The rules were so strict, so hampering at times, it was sweet to see, for once, just once, the letter of the law interpreted to the woman's advantage.

But when, days, weeks, months later, news of the result of that refusal reached those women in their own palaces, or caught up with their jogging camel trains as they made their way towards their distant homes, they would feel a shock untinged by envy, a creeping sense of fear and insecurity. For apparently in this man-made, man-governed world a woman might still adhere to all the rules, behave with the utmost propriety, and yet come to grief. Vashti, queen of the Persians, lately so securely enshrined in the palace and gardens of Shushan, the most beautiful and enviable woman in the world, had been deposed, and all on account of her refusal to show herself, royally robed and crowned, before a crowd of her husband's drunken guests.

It was the men, the husbands of the women who had been

shocked and amused and now were startled, who had brought this thing about. Left to himself, Ahasuerus would have recovered from his anger, and next day, sober, would have apologised to Vashti for his unconventional suggestion. He was deeply in love with her and thought her the fairest among women. Forgiveness would have come easily. But his guests, from two motives, had deliberately fanned his anger and forced him into a decision which he subsequently regretted.

From self-interest they flattered him, as the Danish courtiers flattered Canute some centuries later. They vied with one another to be the foremost to point out that a king who was so great and powerful, who ruled from India to Ethiopia, could not brook insult even from his own queen. And in self-defence they hastened to point out that the story—now known to so many women—would have a bad effect upon behaviour in a thousand harems. If Queen Vashti could, with impunity, defy her husband, how could any man hope to rule his own house? "Thus," they said, "there shall arise too much contempt and wrath." The old fear, the fear known to all who exercise unreasonable power over others, ran high that night, and before Ahasuerus had had a chance to think over the matter coolly they had suggested to him a course which, put into practice, would make every woman in the one hundred and twenty-seven provinces of the vast empire tremble.

Ahasuerus' anger died away and he was left to realise that his revenge had not hurt only Vashti. Without her he was miserable, and his depression affected his courtiers who cast round for some means of lightening it. The plan upon which they finally decided, and which they produced for their monarch's approval, sounds like something out of an Oriental fairy tale. Messengers—they suggested—should be sent out into every province of that wide empire with instructions to bring back to Shushan the most beautiful virgins they could find. Each girl, after undergoing a ritual of preparation was to spend a night in the king's apartment, and the one in whom he took most pleasure should be crowned with Vashti's crown.

After all these intervening centuries the imagination quickens with an echo of the excitement that ran through every province in that vast empire once the scheme was made public. In Babylon and Nineveh, in Memphis, and Petra, and Palmyra, the hope of an impossible day-dream coming true, beat, not only in the breasts of a thousand virgins, but in the minds of their parents and guardians, of generals who had been defeated, politicians who had been outwitted, great kings who had been reduced to tributaries. Upon the shoulders of a single lovely girl a family, a tribe, a whole subjected nation might climb to favour; prestige and power and wealth might be in the gift of any little slender hand.

It is easy to believe that behind the veils and the curtains of the closely guarded litters that began to make their way into Shushan the loveliest faces from every race and tribe were hidden. What else the veils concealed one prefers not to think upon, the home-sickness and the terror, the memory of promises broken and young lovers left behind, the resolute ambitions, the dark erotic wisdom hastily imparted.

Amongst the self-appointed priests ready to offer a virgin upon the altar of one man's self-indulgent whim, was a member of the captive race, a Jew, Mordecai of the tribe of Benjamin. Years before he had adopted his much younger cousin, an orphan, a girl of good lineage and superb beauty, and he had brought her up to the age of fifteen years. Now he saw a possibility of gaining, not only an unhoped-for settlement for his poor relative but an ambassador in the very court of Persia. Esther herself had no choice in the matter, Mordecai was her nearest male relative and she was bound by iron custom, as well as gratitude, to obey him until she found a new master in her husband. With strict instructions that she was not to mention her race, Mordecai delivered her over to Hegai, the king's eunuch who had charge of all the virgins.

One by one the candidates for queenship were bathed and perfumed and robed, given anything in the way of special decoration or toilet requisite that their fancy demanded and led across the garden into the king's apartment. There they did their best with the beauty and charm which nature and art had bestowed upon them, and then returned, still uncertain as to their fate, to await the king's decision. Unparalleled concentration of femininity and rivalry!

It was a year before Esther took her turn and every morning during that year Mordecai came to the palace to inquire about her. But at last the day came when Esther was to seek the king's favour.

Why he preferred her to all the others no authority gives the slightest indication. He must, by that time, have been satiated by mere beauty. Women of every kind and colour had crossed that garden, ivory-skinned beauties from Georgia, ebony-skinned beauties from Ethiopia, palace-bred, delicate-limbed princesses from ruined palaces in conquered kingdoms, sunburnt, strong-bodied shepherdesses, the pick of the nomad tribes. Surely Ahasuerus had had his fill of beauty. And the edge of his lust must have been dulled, too, in that year. What was there so special about the young Jewess?

Invincible romanticism suggests that she most nearly resembled the banished but still-mourned Vashti. And the idea that the two women had something in common is borne out later in the story. Vashti refused to come when she was bidden; Esther dared death by entering the royal presence unbidden. They shared a kind of intrepidity. Esther's feat of courage was still a thing of the future, but some slight hint of it is given in the fact—which the historian seems to think unusual enough to deserve merit—that when her turn came to go to Ahasuerus she made no demand for special clothes or adornments but faced the test in the ordinary regulation harem wear. It may even have been that, despite Mordecai's hopes, she did not much want to be queen of Persia and her lack of ambition may have been reflected in her behaviour. Ahasuerus, tired of flattery and sycophancy, may have relished, as tyrants often do, a glimmer of a spirit unsubdued. He was a man, with a man's innate lust for conquest, and with his ready-made empire and his slavish courtiers it is possible that the only challenge he ever met came from the personalities of the two women he loved, Vashti and Esther, both of whom offered the satiated man "fresh worlds to conquer." For this reason, or for some other, unrecorded and now lost, unguessable in the mists of time, Esther was chosen out of all those hundreds of women, and was crowned. The Jews were captives in a far land; but a Jewess sat upon the throne.

Mordecai, meanwhile, in keeping an eye upon his cousin's progress, had not been wasting his time. He was a gossip, and being a despised Jew, was forced to gossip with his kind. One of these, a palace servant, a humble man, not named, one day whispered a secret in Mordecai's ear. A bit of gossip, interesting, but not important; did the enslaved Jews care whether Ahasuerus ruled or another? And could the servant guess that this sedate old Jew who hung about the precincts of the palace was related to the queen? So he whispered that two of the king's intimates, one of whom was his own master, were hatching one of those palace plots so common in Eastern history. They planned to assassinate Ahasuerus. Mordecai, without a betraying sign, received this piece of information and passed it on to Esther who told her husband. Inquiries were made and the conspirators' guilt was proved and they were hanged. (Josephus adds "upon a cross" which, in the light of history, is an interesting fragment). Esther loyally mentioned Mordecai by name, but the hoped-for reward was not forthcoming though his name and the service he had rendered went into the official records where they lay unremembered for nine years.

Of Esther's life during that nine years we are told nothing. She bore no child—for the historian would never have overlooked this injection of Jewish blood into that of the royal house of Persia. That she had rivals within the women's palace is clearly indicated, but none of them was important enough to be named. The story leaps ahead to the struggle for supremacy between Esther and Haman, between the queen and the favourite: and that was, in miniature, the old struggle between Israel and the Amalekites, fought out this time, not upon the plains of Esdraelon, but in the palace, over the heart, of the king of Persia.

Ahasuerus had found in Haman, the Amalekite, a favourite with whom he was so infatuated that he raised him above all the princes and satraps and made him the second man in the kingdom. He issued—without necessity—an order that everybody was to treat Haman with respect and reverence. Courtiers and princes of the blood, concealing their envy and chagrin, did the favourite homage, and waited for him to make a false step, to bore or offend his master. But Haman's prosperity continued and increased until he was so pampered that a single small slight to his pride assumed a ridiculous proportion like the pea which caused the fairy-tale princess such discomfort through six feather mattresses.

The slight came from someone who should have been beneath Haman's notice, an old Jew who for reasons of his own, haunted the precincts of the palace, the scene of Haman's completest triumph. Mordecai, ill-clad, without position, member of a race held in bondage, refused, obstinately, to give the favourite what he had come to regard as his due. A hint is given, in Haman's vicious hatred of the whole race, that Mordecai may not have been alone in refusing to flatter the Amalekite; but Mordecai was the one whom Haman saw every day, the one Jew who for some obscure reason hung about the palace of the king of Persia: and it was for Mordecai's impassive face and unbowed head that Haman grew to watch and wait; it was Mordecai whom Haman hated most of all.

Worldly and unworldly motives met and mingled in Mordecai's attitude. The Amalekites were one of the tribes who had resisted the Jewish conquest of Palestine: they were old, old enemies against whom Jehovah had always uttered, and worked, ill things. Some strong national feeling lay behind Mordecai's contempt. But there was more. There was, to the strict Jew, a point, frequently reached, where abject adulation to a human being began to savour of an encroachment upon holy ground, a sin against the first commandment. Even to their own kings, men whom they regarded as chosen by God, the Jews were never reverential. With singular ease Mordecai refrained from offering to the Amalekite favourite of the Persian king any shadow of the respect that should be God's alone. He "bowed not, nor did him reverence."

Haman, with the swollen, tender-skinned vanity of the swiftly successful, noted the omission, brooded over it and was finally so obsessed with it that the silence of Mordecai, the Jew, rang louder than all the plaudits and flatteries of the conformers. The only thing he noticed as he passed through Shushan and entered the palace was that one unbowed head. And the farcical situation so preyed upon his mind that as his power increased—that power which in its degree corrupts, little or much, its possessor—he could think of only one way to employ it. He must exterminate, not merely Mordecai, but all his race.

Haman is the first recorded person to make this his objective. Even the Pharaoh who brought the plagues upon Egypt had contented himself with ordering the massacre of male babies; Nebuchadnezzar had merely carried away the whole nation into captivity; the various tribes in Canaan had merely resisted the Jewish invasion. Haman was the first person to plan the destruction of the entire race.

He began by persuading Ahasuerus that the presence of the Jews in the provinces of the empire was a threat to that empire's well-being. Ahasuerus, doting upon his favourite, gave, without protest or interest, his consent to the massacre. Haman lost no time; riders on swift horses set out for given destinations in every one of the one hundred and twenty-seven provinces, just as they had done nine years earlier, but this time they carried, not an invitation to possible queenship, but signed and sealed orders to the provincial governors that upon a certain date all Jews, their wives and children, were to be slain. Haman wanted, one morning, to wake up and remember Mordecai and be able to think that not one Jew was alive in the whole of Persia.

Mordecai, loitering and gossiping, caught the first rumour of the plan and rent his clothes. There was no wailing wall, with its accumulated sorrows and reliefs, in Shushan: that had been left behind, with a thousand other things, in Jerusalem, but the streets of Shushan were not blind or deaf to him. Swift feet ran, swift tongues whispered to Esther and she sent out new garments to replace his rent ones and demanded to know the cause of his grief. Mordecai sent back the garments with a copy of the decree which was already posted up in Shushan and which would go up, day by day, in an ever-widening circle as horseman after horseman reached his destination. And he told her that she was the only person who could save her people. She must go in to Ahasuerus and beg him to cancel the order.

Esther's answer sheds a sinister light upon life in an Eastern palace; the titles and the jewels fall away and the slavery of queenship is revealed, starkly. Appalled as she was by the news she could only send back word that she was helpless. Nobody was allowed to enter the presence of Ahasuerus unbidden; to do so was to invite death; and in that place of lesser wives and concubines it was thirty days since she had seen her husband. She could not see him, therefore she could not plead.

Mordecai sent back another message, ominous, three-fanged. He believed, he said, that even if Esther did not act the Jews would be saved, by some other means, but her family would not share the salvation. Then he reminded her that for nine years she had enjoyed the rank and privilege appertaining to royalty, not through any merit of her own but by a provision of Providence against this very crisis. And finally he pointed out that she was a Jewess, equally under the threat of doom. "Think not with thyself that thou shalt escape in the king's house more than all the Jews." Who, other than himself, was in a position to betray her, Mordecai did not say, but perhaps he was shrewd enough to know that in a purge such as Haman was planning secrets like Esther's had a way of leaking out.

This time the eunuch, Hatach, weaving his way between the old Jew in his mourning clothes and the queen, silk-clad and perfumed, carried a message which satisfied Mordecai. Esther promised that she would force her way into the presence of Ahasuerus and plead for her people. The message ended, "And if I perish, I perish."

That sentence has, despite its almost lyrical tenseness, a melodramatic ring which the modern Western mind accepts with a slight cynicism. Was the favourite queen of nine years' standing really endangering her life by disregarding so arbitrary a rule of court etiquette? Was it likely that Ahasuerus would order the destruction of the woman he had preferred above all others merely because she had entered his presence uninvited? We remind ourselves that Esther thought so, and she knew her world, her court and her husband better than we can. The Eastern potentate, fantastically spoiled, was fantastically fickle. Fawning courtiers, each seeking to outstrip the others in adulation, had forced the prestige of royalty so high that there was no clear line between it and divinity. And in Esther's case there was the ever present memory of Vashti who had lost her crown for an offence incomparably less, since Vashti had been obeying the letter of the law.

It is impossible for us justly to estimate Esther's position. She knew—as we cannot—the significance of those thirty days during which she had not looked upon Ahasuerus' face, though only a garden lay between their apartments. But we can imagine the ghost of the banished Vashti looking out of the silver mirror before which Esther dressed her hair; standing by her shoulder as she put on the glittering crown; following her down the pillared corridor and across the sun-and-shade checkered garden as she made her way to the king's court. Nine years before Esther had taken this same path, undecked, either confident in her young beauty or indifferent to her reception. Did she remember that now? Failure to please Ahasuerus then had meant only that she would return to Mordecai's little house and to the quiet life of exile: failure to please him now meant that she and all her race would die violently, bloodily.

Some versions of the story attempt to heighten the drama of the moment of her intrusion by saying that Ahasuerus looked at her severely. The Bible simply states that when he saw her she obtained favour in his sight. The two aspects are not necessarily in contradiction. The phrase "obtained favour" does suggest that some change occurred in the mind of Ahasuerus when he looked at her, that the favour was not hers at the moment when she stepped within the door. There is, indeed, in the whole of this part of the story, a hint, mainly conveyed by things left unsaid, that the first romantic attraction had waned. Nine years is a long time in the favour of a fickle monarch with the beauties of half the world at his command, nine years is a long time in the beauty of a woman, especially in the East.

But, now that she had forced herself upon him, the old spell, after a wavering, uncertain moment during which Esther's head was in peril, held. Ahasuerus stretched out towards her the golden sceptre that he held in his hand, and that was an acknowledged sign that the intrusion was pardoned and the intruder given the right to speak.

Here was a moment equally perilous. If one feels that Esther deserves little credit for her action in entering the presence since she was forced and threatened into it by Mordecai, one cannot deny her admiration for her skill in handling this, psychologically, even more dangerous moment. So many women, remembering those blank thirty days and granted this fleeting opportunity would have there and then fallen upon their knees and in a muddled spate of relief and hysteria and supplication poured out their request. Esther, more skilled, or more sure of herself, proffered, with a lightness oddly incongruous with the danger she had just escaped, an invitation that Ahasuerus and his favourite should attend a banquet which she had prepared for them in her apartments. Ahasuerus, also remembering those blank thirty days, could hardly fail to be pleased and flattered at the realisation that she had risked her life in order to ask him to a feast. He accepted with alacrity.

A question here forces itself forward, unjustified perhaps by the text, but imaginatively urgent. Had the slight coolness between the king and queen had its origin in Haman? Both the king, urging Haman to make haste to attend, and Haman boasting of the invitation to his wife, seem to regard the apparently ordinary social gesture as something of extraordinary significance. Had Esther, almost unconsciously, scented the Amalekite, or been jealous of him, and displeased Ahasuerus by hitherto ignoring his pet?

But now the breach—if breach there had been—was closed and the two men enjoyed the feast which was set before them. Ahasuerus was so delighted—by the meal? by the reunion?—that he promised Esther, in the phrase that has become a by-word anything she asked "even to the half of the kingdom." And Esther, again exercising restraint, said that the only thing she had to ask was that they should feast with her again on the next day. She was fortunate in that she had time to move delicately. Mordecai, in the heart of the empire, was already aware of doom and mourning in sackcloth and ashes, but the day appointed for the massacre was still some way ahead and upon the outskirts of the kingdom the messengers were still urging their horses forward and the order was still folded in their wallets.

The king and his favourite accepted the invitation to the second feast and Haman went home to erect—at his wife's suggestion—the gallows upon which he meant to hang Mordecai, the sight of whose unbowed head on his way home from the palace had been sufficient to tarnish the sparkle of an evening spent alone in the company of the king and queen.

The idea of building a gallows—higher than ordinary—for his enemy, soothed Haman and he slept, but Ahasuerus for some reason was wakeful, and since the lonely hours of insomnia were not to be borne by the king of Persia, a scribe came to read to him, and the scribe chose, of all things, the dusty roll which recorded the now nearly forgotten story of the palace plot which Mordecai had exposed. Almost too timely to be an accident the coincidence that in the same night Ahasuerus should be reminded that the man who had saved his life had gone unrewarded, while Haman dreamed of a tall gallows from which that same man should swing.

Haman came early to the palace next morning and Ahasuerus greeted him with the question, "What shall be done to the man whom the king delighteth to honour?" Haman, the egocentric, could think of no man fitting that description but himself and he suggested an honour which he coveted, speaking aloud a cherished dream. Let that man, he said, put on the royal robes and the crown of Persia and mount the horse which ordinarily carried no one but the king, and let him, so clad, so mounted, go through the streets of Shushan, preceded by a herald who would announce to the people that this was the man whom the king delighted to favour. Had Haman not been already doomed for a more spectacular fall, the suggestion might have brought him down. Did Ahasuerus reflect that as a man dreams so he is, and smile into his curled black beard as he gravely accepted the preposterous suggestion and said, "Make haste and do even so to Mordecai, the Jew; let nothing fail of all that thou hast spoken."

Haman was still in his house, mourning the day's humiliation, when the chamberlains came to conduct him to Esther's second feast. The wines, the food, the company were just the same as on the previous evening; even fragments of conversation were the same, for again Ahasuerus asked Esther her pleasure, offering her anything she cared to name, even to the half of the kingdom. But now the hour had struck. Esther proffered her startling request and begged for the lives of her people and for her own life which some enemy was plotting to destroy. Ahasuerus, startled by this sudden introduction of stark tragedy into the middle of a joyous feast, demanded to know the name of this enemy. Esther lifted her jewelled hand and pointed across the table to the place where Haman lolled.

Ahasuerus knew that he faced an awkward and unpleasant situation, and his pampered spirit shrank from it. He made a childish attempt to convert his escape impulse into physical action, and rose and flung himself into the palace garden, leaving Esther and Haman alone together. But even in the garden Ahasuerus could not avoid the necessity to decide, now, between his queen and his favourite, nor escape the knowledge that the order for the massacre had borne his name and his seal and gone out with his approval. When Haman had made his infamous suggestion, the Jews had been nothing to Ahasuerus, a few hundreds of aliens, an unwanted legacy from Babylonia to Persia, their names unknown, their customs incomprehensible. It had been easy then to believe that they were dangerous and revolutionary and better out of the way. But now, after Esther's startling confession, these shadowy people emerged from anonymity and stood represented by two persons for whom the king had liking and respect, the grave old man, Mordecai, who had saved his life nine years ago and only this morning received recognition for the service, and the lovely woman, Esther, whom he had chosen before all others to be his wife.

Opposed to them was the favourite, Haman. What he offered, of amusement or charm for his master has never been told, but there must have been something which the king valued, some mental support or spiritual release or physical attraction. Even his self-aggrandisement and posturings may have afforded Ahasuerus a vast, secret amusement. But already the scale of favour was turning against Haman, and it may have been tilted by his aggressive suggestion that morning. The royal robes, the royal charger, the royal crown. Ahasuerus must have known then that Haman's ambition was limitless and could go no further without becoming dangerous. Whereas Esther, even when driven to desperate means, had retained a mean demeanour, a tacit, tactful knowledge of her subordinate position. It was Haman who must go.

If there had been the least lingering doubt in the king's mind it was dispersed by the sight which met his eyes when he returned to the banqueting chamber. Haman, in abject terror, had begun to beg Esther for her forgiveness and support and was grovelling upon the ground by the couch where she reclined, his frenzied hands clutching at hers, at her robes, at her knees. Ahasuerus had not seen or guessed that Haman was extremely frightened; (and this suggests that Haman's favour may have originated in his ability to interpret his master's mood almost before he himself knew it) and, finding him thus, bellowed out a furious accusation of amorous assault. The chamberlains came running. The one person who could have cleared Haman of that charge, at least, uttered no word. Esther sat silent. She knew why Haman had thrown himself upon her; but she knew also that if she spoke Ahasuerus, in violent reaction, might take Haman back into favour and sacrifice the Jews. Hers is one of the most significant silences in history. One of the chamberlains mentioned, as if casually, the tall gallows which had been reared for Mordecai, and Ahasuerus, with the same precipitance with which he had snatched the crown from Vashti, ordered that Haman should be hanged thereon immediately.

The story ends with this complete turning of tables; with another set of post-riders galloping off to the one hundred and twenty-seven provinces to cancel the order for the massacre; with Mordecai clad in royal apparel and with "a great crown of gold," with Esther's influence over the king again unchallenged and with every exiled Jew keeping high festival. Small wonder that some historians judged it to belong to the realm of fiction rather than fact. For the others—those who hold that truth can be stranger than fiction—there is the evidence of the Feast of Purim, that memorial day of rejoicing which celebrates the triumph of Esther and takes its name from the word *Pur*—the *lot* which Haman cast when he tried to destroy an indestructible race.

"The high song is over. Silent is the lute now,
  They are crowned forever and discrowned now,
Whether they triumphed or suffered they are mute now,
  Or at the most they are only a sound now.

"There is no need for blame, no cause for praise now.
  Nothing to hide, to change or to discover.
They were men and women. They have gone their ways now,
  As men and women must. The high song is over."

(*Humbert Wolfe*: REQUIEM)